RUM, BLOOD & TREASURE

RUM, BLOOD & TREASURE

Stories Strange and True from Atlantic Canada

EDWARD BUTTS

Formac Publishing Company Limited
Halifax

Formac Publishing Company Limited recognizes the support of the Province of Nova Scotia through Film and Creative Industries Nova Scotia. We are pleased to work in partnership with the Province of Nova Scotia to develop and promote our creative industries for the benefit of all Nova Scotians. We acknowledge the support of the Canada Council for the Arts, which last year invested $157 million to bring the arts to Canadians throughout the country.

Cover design: Meredith Bangay
Cover image: Shutterstock

Library and Archives Canada Cataloguing in Publication
Butts, Edward, 1951-, author
        Rum, blood & treasure : stories strange but true from Atlantic Canada
/ Edward Butts.

Includes bibliographical references and index.
Issued in print and electronic formats.
ISBN 978-1-4595-0414-1 (paperback).--ISBN 978-1-4595-0415-8 (epub)

        1. Atlantic Provinces--History. 2. Curiosities and wonders--Atlantic
Provinces. I. Title. II. Title: Rum, blood and treasure.

FC2005.B88 2016   971.5   C2015-907666-8
                                            C2015-907667-6

Formac Publishing Company Limited
5502 Atlantic Street
Halifax, Nova Scotia, Canada
B3H 1G4
www.formac.ca

Printed and bound in Canada.

To the memory of Tom Butts of Florence, Cape Breton:
miner, Great Lakes sailor, Coastguardsman,
and the greatest uncle ever.

Table of Contents

Introduction

As the son of a Cape Breton–born man, I have always been fascinated by the history and lore of Atlantic Canada. In other books I've written about Canadian crime, police, battles, and disasters, I've always ensured that the Atlantic Provinces are fairly represented. Presented with the opportunity to do a book specifically on the East Coast, I decided to tell some of the stories that aren't as universally known.

The bitter and bloody feud between Charles La Tour and Charles d'Aulnay in Acadia presents us with an aspect of colonialism often overlooked in history textbooks: the pursuit of wealth and power that pitted individuals rather than nations against each other. Though the story of treasure hunting on Nova Scotia's Oak Island has been thoroughly documented, few people are aware that the deadly sandbars of Sable Island claimed as one of its many victims a ship carrying the costly personal equipage of a prince.

Through the eyes of a humble servant named John Paul Radelmüller, we get a look into the private, often scandalous lives of the ruling class. Charles Coghlan was one of the most famous actors of his time, and in an age before gossip magazines, his affairs set tongues wagging. But it was his connection to Prince Edward Island and the strange circumstances surrounding his untimely death that have made him the subject of a century-old mystery. The story of the Kellums, a family in nineteenth-century Halifax's black community, is one of pathos, irony, and an unusual turn on the ingenuity of human struggle for survival.

Prohibition-era rum-runners became folk heroes in the lore of Atlantic Canada. Historians of the period are familiar with the controversial sinking of the schooner *I'm Alone* by the United States Coast Guard. However, not many people today know of the personal account of the *I'm Alone*'s captain, war hero and adventurer Jack Randell of Newfoundland. Fewer still know the tale of the *Josephine K*, whose otherwise law-abiding, church-going skipper met a violent death as a smuggler. I thought it fair to include a chapter on the French island of Saint-Pierre since it played such a prominent role in Prohibition-era rum-running. The Saint-Pierre story presented here has a surprising, if admittedly tenuous, Canadian connection.

Murder both horrifies and fascinates us. In cases presented here from across the Maritimes, we have everything from a perplexing Cape Breton mystery, to a crime solved by an observant investigator, to poignant scenarios that stand as arguments against capital punishment. Prince Edward Island might seem an unlikely place for the capture of Canada's most-wanted bank robber, but the arrest under dramatic circumstance is a matter of record, long buried in the archives of local newspapers.

The stories in this book are accounts of extraordinary events. They come from the unique history and lore of Atlantic Canada, but have a place in the collective chronicles of the nation. I hope readers will find these stories surprising and intriguing.

PART I

TREACHERY AND MYSTERY

1

The La Tours:
Treachery in Acadia

The Acadian Civil War was one of the bloodiest episodes in the early history of Nova Scotia and New Brunswick. Taking place amidst the larger French–English conflict, it was a vicious struggle between rival French colonizers. Central to the dramatic events was Charles de Sainte-Étienne de La Tour, an ambitious rogue whose life had all the elements of a romantic swashbuckling adventure.

In 1610, seventeen-year-old La Tour sailed from Dieppe, France, to Acadia with his father Claude. They were with an expedition led by Jean de Biencourt de Poutrincourt de Saint-Just, who intended to re-establish Samuel de Champlain's colony at Port Royal (now Annapolis Royal). That settlement, founded in 1604, had failed because of financial difficulties. The La Tours had been there from 1606 until it was abandoned in 1607.

Young La Tour loved the wilds of the New World. In his free time he would fish and hunt, pursuits that were only for the aristocracy in France. Fur trading was the colony's principal economic activity, and La Tour became friendly with the Mi'kmaq trappers. Soon he could speak their language.

Charles La Tour was excited to be in Port Royal, but Poutrincourt's plans for revitalizing the colony would not go well. Maintaining the settlement was expensive, and fur smuggling deprived Poutrincourt of badly needed funds. In 1612, young La Tour was involved in a fight with a poacher's ship, and in November 1613, while Poutrincourt was in France, an English force from Virginia sacked Port Royal. Some of the surviving colonists set off on an arduous overland journey for the new French settlements on the St. Lawrence River. The La Tours and a few others went to live with the Mi'kmaq.

Poutrincourt returned in the spring of 1614 and saw the desolation. The destruction of Port Royal broke him both financially and in spirit. He sailed back to France, taking with him any disheartened settlers who'd had enough. But the La Tours and a handful of others still saw possibilities in Acadia and stayed.

Over the next few years, the tough colonists bartered with Mi'kmaq for furs and partially rebuilt Port Royal. Periodically ships arrived from France with supplies and trade goods, leaving with holds full of pelts that were fetching increasingly higher prices in Europe. In one year, more than 25,000 pelts of beaver, otter, marten, moose, and deer were shipped from Acadia.

In about 1626, Claude La Tour returned to France on one of the supply ships, and shortly after, Charles established a post on Cap de Sable off Nova Scotia's southeast coast. He called it Fort Lomeron in honour of David Lomeron, his partner and agent, and it soon became a thriving fur trade centre. La Tour established outposts on the Nova Scotia mainland and cracked down on fur poachers. He was the leader of Acadia in everything but title. He knew the country and had important contacts in France. La Tour had also married a Mi'kmaq woman, whose name was not recorded, with whom he had three daughters.

In 1627, England and France were again at war. Charles wrote letters to King Louis XIII and his chief minister Cardinal de Richelieu explaining that with little help from France, he had held Acadia by training a company of Frenchmen and natives to harass English intruders. Now, Charles pleaded, he needed supplies, reinforcements, and an official commission authorizing him to defend Acadia. La Tour sent the letters to his father in Paris, who personally delivered them to the king and Richelieu.

In the spring of 1628, Claude La Tour sailed from France with a fleet of four ships. But en route to Acadia, they were waylaid by the English privateer Sir David Kirke. Claude was taken to England as a prisoner. No help from France reached Acadia that year or the next.

During his incarceration, Claude was won over to the English side with promises of wealth and position. When two English warships arrived at Cap de Sable in the spring of 1630, Claude was with them. He went ashore and tried to convince his son to surrender Fort Lomeron, for which Charles would be well rewarded. According to reports, Charles told his father that "he would rather have died than consent to such baseness as to betray his king." Claude returned to his ship.

The English attacked Fort Lomeron, but the assault failed. Licking their wounds, the English withdrew to a new post they had established near the ruins of Port Royal. Because Claude had failed to deliver Fort Lomeron, the English did not deliver on their promises to him. He eventually returned to the French side, was granted clemency, and reconciled with his son. Claude lived in the home Charles provided for him on Cap de Sable.

When news of Charles' successful defence of Fort Lomeron reached Paris, Louis XIII officially made him Governor of Acadia and sent him men and supplies. In 1631, La Tour decided that the best location for a trading post was a site at the mouth of the St. John River, almost directly across the Bay of Fundy from Port Royal. The new post, called Fort Sainte-Marie-de-Grâce, drew a wealth of furs, second only to Quebec. At one point, Scottish settlers from Port Royal attacked the fort and plundered it. La Tour retaliated by capturing and pillaging an English post at Machias, Maine. He then repaired the damage done to Fort Sainte-Marie-de-Grâce, which was known thereafter as Fort La Tour.

For years, Charles La Tour had been working and fighting in Acadia in the interests of France — and himself. He had held off the English and gained the office of governor. But Acadia was far from Paris, where the power struggles and intrigues of the French court could have widespread and long-lasting consequences. Cardinal de Richelieu, a scheming and ambitious man whose power almost equalled the king's, cast an avaricious eye on the lucrative Acadian fur trade.

In 1632, Richelieu's cousin, Isaac de Razilly, arrived in Acadia with official documents naming him Lieutenant General and Governor of New France, which included Acadia. His second-in-command was another Richelieu kinsman, Charles de Menou d'Aulnay. The large company of men Razilly had brought with him forced the Scottish settlers to abandon Port Royal, which certainly suited La Tour. But Razilly's documented authority as governor clashed with La Tour's, and Charles sailed to France to sort the matter out.

Louis XIII heard La Tour's case and conferred with Richelieu. They worked out a compromise. Razilly would be in command at Port Royal and La Tour would command Fort La Tour and keep Cap de Sable. The two would otherwise share in the exploitation of Acadia's resources. As a precaution against cheating, each could keep two clerks in the other's headquarters to watch what was going into warehouses and onto ships. While in France, La Tour recruited new colonists.

When La Tour returned to Acadia in the spring of 1633, he found Razilly favourable to the new arrangement of shared governorship. Razilly was an amiable and honourable man who respected La Tour. For two years, the men worked well together and Acadia thrived. Then in 1635, Razilly died suddenly at the age of forty-eight. Command of Port Royal passed to his first lieutenant, d'Aulnay.

Born around 1604, d'Aulnay was an aristocrat whose father had been a councillor to Louis XIII. D'Aulnay had been a captain in the French navy and, as Razilly's right-hand man at Port Royal, had even fought alongside La Tour against the English. But d'Aulnay looked upon La Tour as an inferior. It offended his pride and sense of social order that he should have to share authority — and profits — with a commoner as though they were equals.

After Razilly's death, La Tour had hoped that Port Royal would be restored to him. He was resentful that it had gone to d'Aulnay. No doubt it rankled La Tour when d'Aulnay poached seals from his territory of Cap de Sable.

D'Aulnay was in turn infuriated when in 1636, Claude de La Tour was granted his own trading post and a seigneury at Fort Pentagouet, which d'Aulnay had seized from the English in 1635. Although Claude probably died within a year (his name vanishes from record after 1636) the incident deepened d'Aulnay's hatred of Charles La Tour.

Over the next three years, La Tour and d'Aulnay evidently clashed several times. Each wrote to France, pleading his own case and complaining about the other. Once again Louis XIII and Richelieu, concerned that trouble in Acadia would diminish profits, came up with a compromise, but it was a clumsy one that was doomed to failure.

A letter from the king arrived in Acadia in 1638. It revealed a poor understanding of the disputed territory's geography. The royal document gave La Tour authority over peninsular Acadia (Nova Scotia), but not Port Royal. It gave d'Aulnay the lands north of the Bay of Fundy (New Brunswick), but not Fort La Tour. The rivals now operated from headquarters that were surrounded by land in the other's jurisdiction. Further complicating the arrangement was the king's order that La Tour and d'Aulnay cooperate in sharing administrative costs and allow access to each other's post, just as had been done when La Tour worked with Razilly.

By this time, d'Aulnay had married Jeanne Motin, a young woman who had travelled to Acadia with her father Louis, one of d'Aulnay's business partners. Taking a wife was a clear indication that d'Aulnay intended to put down roots in Acadia. The couple would have eight children.

There is no record of what became of La Tour's Mi'kmaq wife. He had taken two of his daughters to France with him and put them into convents to be educated and the third remained in Acadia.

La Tour needed a French wife to give him legitimate heirs. However, due to concerns about d'Aulnay, he couldn't go to France himself. So in 1639, La Tour sent one of his senior officers, Guillaume Desjardins, to bring him back a suitable spouse. La Tour might have already had someone in particular in mind, but Desjardins had written authority to select a bride he thought would be a good match. That would mean a woman who would not wilt under the rigours of colonial life.

In 1640, Desjardins returned to Acadia with Françoise-Marie Jacquelin. It's possible that La Tour had met her when he was in Paris. Almost nothing is known of her early life. According to one account, her father was a lowly barber, and she was an actress in the theatres of Paris. More likely, her father was Dr. Jacques Jacquelin, a member of the lesser nobility. Whatever her origins, Françoise-Marie was to play a dramatic role in Acadia's history.

La Tour married Françoise-Marie in a formal Catholic ceremony, and they moved into a comfortable house he had built. However, the ship that brought the bride to her new husband also carried a cargo of arms and ammunition. Françoise-Marie soon realized that her husband was about to go to war with a fellow Frenchman.

When natives killed two of d'Aulnay's traders on the St. John River, d'Aulnay was certain that La Tour was behind the attack. Then La Tour captured two of d'Aulnay's small coastal vessels and put the crews to work on his fort's defences. D'Aulnay, retaliated, but documentation of his actions has been lost.

Soon after, La Tour decided to take Françoise-Marie across the bay to Port Royal. The pretext for this unusual social call was to introduce his new wife to Jeanne, but La Tour actually wanted to look in d'Aulnay's warehouses.

When La Tour arrived at Port Royal, he was refused admittance. He took this as an insult to him and his wife. D'Aulnay had broken the code of honour. The standoff exploded into a sea battle in the Annapolis Basin. Both leaders would claim that the other fired the first shot.

Cannons roared, ships' timbers were blasted to splinters, and men on both sides were killed and wounded. La Tour put up a spirited fight, but d'Aulnay was the more experienced sea captain. D'Aulnay won the battle and took La Tour and Françoise-Marie prisoner along with their surviving crewmen.

According to the code of chivalry, Françoise-Marie should have been treated with courtesy. Instead, d'Aulnay called her La Tour's "mistress" and had her imprisoned with her husband. The experience was unpleasant and humiliating.

D'Aulnay seemed content to hold his prisoners indefinitely, but Capuchin friars persuaded him to refer the matter to the king. Together, La Tour and d'Aulnay drew up and signed a peace bond, after which d'Aulnay released the captives.

Françoise-Marie had been through a baptism of fire she had not anticipated when she left France. But she was no shrinking violet. On the voyage back to Fort La Tour, she assured her husband that she would stand by him come what may. She may well have made a private oath never again to fall into d'Aulnay's hands.

La Tour and d'Aulnay both sent letters to the king. D'Aulnay's connections at court were stronger, and the royal council decided in his favour. The king's instructions arrived in Acadia in the summer of 1641. La Tour had been stripped of his governorship and was to return to France to explain his "bad behaviour." D'Aulnay was instructed to arrest La Tour if he did not obey. He was to take over La Tour's forts and posts and put them in the charge of men loyal to the king.

La Tour had no intention of returning to France or of giving himself up to d'Aulnay. Because Cap de Sable would have been difficult to defend, he surrendered it to d'Aulnay in what he hoped would appear to the king as a goodwill gesture. Instead of placing the fort in the charge of a reliable man as the king had ordered, d'Aulnay burned it to the ground.

Cut off from French fur markets and badly in need of

supplies, La Tour made a stunning move. He sent one of his lieutenants, Nicolas Gargot de la Rochette, to Boston to negotiate a trade deal with the English and to hire mercenaries. When d'Aulnay got word of this, he sailed to France and accused La Tour of treason.

On an August morning in 1642, d'Aulnay anchored his ship off Fort La Tour. He sent a party of men ashore with a letter from the king. La Tour came to the gate and listened as a spokesman read aloud the long list of charges and the king's direct order for him to return to France immediately. La Tour snatched the paper from the man's hand, crumpled it into a ball, and threw it on the ground. He then took d'Aulnay's men prisoner. D'Aulnay sailed back to Port Royal in a fury.

This time, La Tour knew he could not disobey the king, but he was reluctant to leave with d'Aulnay poised to seize his fort. Françoise-Marie, now the mother of a baby son, was afraid Charles would be imprisoned in France, so she volunteered to go in his place. There were no charges against Françoise-Marie, so she was in no danger of arrest. She sailed in September.

Appearing before the king's court, Françoise-Marie explained that her husband had been unable to make the voyage due to poor health. When she pleaded La Tour's case. Françoise-Marie argued that most of d'Aulnay's charges were exaggerated and even fabricated, and that d'Aulnay had been responsible for the violence. She drew attention to d'Aulnay's destruction of Cap de Sable in violation of the king's orders. Moreover, Françoise-Marie had documents signed by priests in Port Royal, which La Tour had secretly obtained, that stated that all was not well in the settlement. According to those letters, d'Aulnay's autocratic ways had been the cause of much trouble and dissatisfaction.

By this time, Cardinal de Richelieu had died. His replacement, Jean Armand de Maille-Breze, the duc de Fronsac, was much more willing to give Françoise-Marie a fair hearing than the cardinal. She was so persuasive, that the duc de Fronsac reinstated La Tour as governor and gave Françoise-Marie supplies, a company of soldiers, and the use of a ship, the *St. Clement*. She sailed in mid-April 1643.

D'Aulnay's spies in Paris sent him warning. So, when the *St. Clement* hove into view at Fort La Tour, three of d'Aulnay's ships had blockaded the harbour. The fort was under siege, and La Tour had already beaten back an assault.

Under cover of darkness, La Tour slipped past d'Aulnay's fleet in a shallop and reached the *St. Clement*. La Tour had an emotional reunion with Françoise-Marie. Then he convinced the captain to sail to Boston instead of engaging in an uneven sea battle.

Boston's governor, John Winthrop, allowed La Tour to hire four armed ships and sixty-eight mercenaries. This fighting force sailed into the Bay of Fundy in the first week of August. D'Aulnay's ships, still hovering off Fort La Tour, immediately fled to Port Royal with La Tour in pursuit.

Now it was d'Aulnay's turn to bar the gate. La Tour sent him a letter demanding reimbursement for his losses at Cap de Sable. D'Aulnay returned the letter unopened. In frustration, La Tour ordered his mercenaries to set fire to a mill and a cornfield. Three of d'Aulnay's men were killed.

Satisfied that he had done his enemy some damage, La Tour returned to his fort, capturing on the way a small vessel headed to Port Royal with a cargo of furs. The English returned to Boston when their contract expired.

D'Aulnay lost no time in hurrying to Paris. He claimed that La Tour had committed armed rebellion against France, and the fact that La Tour had employed English mercenaries weighed heavily against him. The king's court declared La Tour an outlaw. Once more, d'Aulnay had the legal power to arrest La Tour and anyone who supported him. However, his instructions specifically said that all who surrendered to him were to be given good treatment.

La Tour had anticipated what d'Aulnay would do in France. Once again, reluctantly, he sent Françoise-Marie to Paris. This time her mission failed. Françoise-Marie was not only denied permission to purchase supplies for Fort La Tour, but she was also placed under house arrest and forbidden on pain of death to attempt to leave France.

Françoise-Marie sent La Tour a letter warning him that D'Aulnay had gained the upper hand. Then, at great risk, she escaped to England. In London, Françoise-Marie met Captain Jean Bailey of the merchant ship *Gillyflower* and contracted him for passage home.

Bailey had agreed to take Françoise-Marie straight to Acadia. Instead, he sailed for Newfoundland, and from there went up and down the St. Lawrence, stopping to trade at every post and settlement. Six months after leaving England, the *Gillyflower* was finally off Cap de Sable, headed for the Bay of Fundy when she was intercepted by a French warship. The captain who came aboard to speak to Bailey was d'Aulnay.

D'Aulnay had heard of Françoise-Marie's flight from France. Certain that she would try to return to Fort La Tour, he'd been patrolling the Acadian coast, hoping to capture her. While d'Aulnay stood on the *Gillyflower*'s deck, Françoise-Marie was in the hold, where Bailey had hidden her as soon as he'd seen d'Aulnay's flag.

Bailey told D'Aulnay that he was six months out of London, had been to Newfoundland, and was now bound for Boston. Satisfied that Bailey had nothing to conceal, d'Aulnay left the ship. But Bailey now had no choice but to sail for New England.

In Boston, Françoise-Marie sued Captain Bailey and the owners of the *Gillyflower* for breach of contract. She was awarded two thousand pounds and used the money to hire three ships to take her past d'Aulnay's patrol. She reached Fort La Tour in late December 1643 after an absence of fifteen months.

Once again there was a joyful family reunion. But the situation at Fort La Tour was desperate. The war with d'Aulnay had drained La Tour's finances, and he was in debt to his associates in Boston. His warehouses were almost empty and the settlement was low on food and supplies. Many of his followers had deserted to Port Royal, where d'Aulnay welcomed them with open arms.

While Françoise-Marie was in Boston, she learned that New England merchants were keen to do business with Acadia. Moreover, d'Aulnay himself had corresponded with the English. Françoise-Marie told her husband that he had to go to Boston and convince the English that it would be in their best interest to support him against d'Aulnay because d'Aulnay was untrustworthy. Seeing no other option, and believing that d'Aulnay would not attack during the winter, La Tour set off for Boston in mid-January 1645. He left the fort in the charge of the person he most trusted — Françoise-Marie.

In February, several priests and soldiers defected to Port Royal and told d'Aulnay that La Tour had gone to Boston. The fort was now defended by just forty-five hungry men commanded by a woman.

Bad weather discouraged any military expedition for several weeks. Then, in early April, d'Aulnay's blockade captured a small ship carrying emergency supplies to Fort La Tour from Boston. D'Aulnay learned from the crew that La Tour was raising a large relief force. He decided to strike before reinforcements arrived.

On April 13, 1645, d'Aulnay's warship, the *Grand Cardinal*, sailed into Fort La Tour's harbour with a flotilla of smaller vessels and two hundred men. The sixteen powerful naval cannons on the *Grand Cardinal* alone outnumbered the few small field guns in the fort. D'Aulnay's fleet bombarded Fort La Tour, but Françoise-Marie's gunners replied with a savage barrage that killed twenty men, wounded thirteen, and punched enough holes in the hull of the *Grand Cardinal* to put her in danger of sinking.

D'Aulnay withdrew his fleet from artillery range and took the *Grand Cardinal* to a sheltered point where she could be repaired. During the night, he sent parties ashore to set up gun batteries that could pound the most vulnerable sections of the fort's wooden palisade. The defenders would be caught in the crossfire from land and water.

A few days later, the *Grand Cardinal* approached within shouting distance of the fort. D'Aulnay demanded immediate surrender. Françoise-Marie replied with cannon fire. Her men cheered her and jeered d'Aulnay as they raised a red flag of defiance.

On d'Aulnay's order, cannons roared from both ship and shore, and a rain of iron balls smashed into Fort La Tour. Wooden walls buckled and sagged. Fires broke out, and men had to leave their battle stations to form bucket brigades. The fort's two surgeons worked tirelessly tending bleeding wounds and shattered bones.

Despite inferior numbers and dwindling munitions, the defenders fought hard. Their cannon and musket fire blew back assaults on their walls. Throughout the battle, Françoise-Marie was on the ramparts encouraging the men.

How long the battle lasted isn't certain. D'Aulnay would report that it was one long day, from sunrise to sunset. Others claimed the fighting lasted three days. However, the outcome was never in doubt.

At some point, d'Aulnay withdrew to prepare for a final assault. He had lost men, but still had more than enough to take the fort. He stirred them up with promises of loot.

The sections of the fort's walls made of two-foot-thick stone had withstood the cannon fire, but a gap had been blasted through the palisade. Françoise-Marie stationed a Swiss mercenary named Hans Vandre to keep watch while her exhausted men rested during the unexpected lull. But when Vandre saw the enemy creeping forward, he failed to raise the alarm. He may have been bribed, or he may have realized the garrison was doomed and kept silent in hope of saving his own life.

D'Aulnay's men rushed through the breach. Françoise-Marie roused her men and led them in a charge to repulse the intruders. The fighting was furious and bloody as men battled at close quarters with swords, pikes, and musket butts. The defenders fought with such desperation that they drove the attackers back through the gap.

Then d'Aulnay shouted to Françoise-Marie that if she surrendered, he would spare their lives. Françoise-Marie knew that her handful of soldiers could not withstand another assault. She agreed to d'Aulnay's conditions and told her men to lay down their arms.

D'Aulnay led his victorious men into Fort La Tour. But as soon as he had it secured, he broke his promise and ordered all of Françoise-Marie's surviving soldiers to be hanged. When Françoise-Marie protested, he said he would not have offered terms of surrender if he had known that so few still opposed him. He said he had lost too many of his own men to show mercy.

With a noose tied around her neck, Françoise-Marie was forced to watch in horror as her men were hanged one at a time. Not even the wounded were spared. The only two who were allowed to live were Vandre and one defender who bought his own life by agreeing to execute his comrades.

Françoise-Marie was again d'Aulnay's prisoner. He allowed her the freedom of the fort until she was caught trying to pass a message to a visiting native to take to La Tour. D'Aulnay had her locked up and told her she would be sent to France to stand trial for treason.

Confined to a room in the fort that had once been her home, Françoise-Marie fell ill with a fever and died within a month. That, at least, was what d'Aulnay reported. There were rumours that he had poisoned her.

La Tour was still in Boston when he received the devastating news of Françoise-Marie's death. His fort, all of his possessions, and his little son were in d'Aulnay's hands. (D'Aulnay sent the boy to France after which there is no further record.) Destitute, La Tour borrowed money from friends to leave New England. He eventually made his way to Quebec, where he engaged in the fur trade and gradually recovered financially. He had become a prominent figure in the colony when he was again touched by fate.

Having defeated his greatest enemy, d'Aulnay consolidated his hold on Acadia. He drove out all competitors and ruled the colony as though it were his fiefdom. Then on May 24, 1650, at the age of forty-six, d'Aulnay died from exposure after his canoe overturned in the frigid water of the Annapolis Basin.

When La Tour heard of d'Aulnay's death, he immediately sailed to France. He eloquently argued his case before the royal court and won. The king decided that d'Aulnay had been responsible for all the trouble in Acadia after all.

La Tour triumphantly returned to Port Royal in 1653 with his property and his governorship restored. In a supreme twist of irony, he married d'Aulnay's widow. Though it was a union of convenience that benefited both parties financially and politically, it still produced four children.

Charles de La Tour died in Acadia in the spring of 1663

around the age of seventy. He had lost the final battle with d'Aulnay, but in the end he had won the war. In a conflict rife with duplicity, intrigue, and treachery, only one character emerged as noble — Françoise-Marie, the brave defender of Fort La Tour, a heroine of Acadian history and lore.

2

Sable Island: Prince Edward's Treasure

When King George III ordered Prince Edward Augustus, Duke of Kent, to take command of the armed forces in British North America in 1799, responsibility for overseeing the packing of Edward's property for the voyage fell to his porter, John Paul Radelmüller. It would have been an onerous task and required the work of many servants, because the prince never travelled light. Anticipating a lengthy stay in the colonies, Edward would have to take along all the comforts and luxuries befitting a member of the royal family — items of high quality not available in colonial capitals like Halifax and Quebec City: fine furniture, beautiful carpets and drapes, a library, gilded dinnerware, silver plate, excellent wines and spirits, and all the other things Edward and his constant companion, Julie de St. Laurent, would need to set up house in the style to which they were accustomed.

Among the most valuable "packages" Radelmüller had

to prepare were those that contained Edward's wardrobe and personal effects. The prince had expensive tastes, which was an ongoing sore point in his estranged relationship with his father. Edward's equipage had to be the best. He ran up enormous debts fitting himself out with splendid uniforms, exquisite swords, state-of-the-art firearms, and an array of decorative military accessories.

Edward's riding gear, from boots and spurs to saddles, was top of the line. Edward even took along his coach and several prize English horses that, in addition to providing transportation and recreational riding for the prince and his lady, would be used to improve the breeding stock in the colonies. The bills for all of these ostentatious indulgences landed on the desks of the king's clerks. George III was already sinking into madness, and his son's extravagance may have hastened his decline.

One ship couldn't carry all of Edward's possessions. Some of them went into the hold of the naval frigate *Arethusa*, which left Portsmouth, England, for Halifax on July 25, 1799, with Edward, Julie, and Radelmüller and other servants on board. The rest of his possessions, which included Edward's plate, silverware, and military finery, were on the government transport ship *Francis*. Edward had left this property in the charge of Dr. Copeland, a British Army surgeon who was returning to Halifax with his wife and two children after a visit to England. He was to join the prince's staff as Edward's personal physician.

The *Francis* was to have sailed soon after the *Arethusa*, but a crisis in the war with Napoleon kept her in port until December. The ship finally left England in the season when the North Atlantic gales were at their most severe. The *Francis* was sailing into deadly waters.

Edward resided in Halifax as the guest of Governor Sir John Wentworth. He would have learned from visiting Royal Navy captains that the departure of the *Francis* had been delayed. Later, the prince would have heard that the *Francis* had sailed from the commander of a swift Royal Navy vessel that left England sometime after the *Francis*, and arrived in Halifax well before the slower transport ship could make the crossing.

For weeks Edward waited, anticipating that any day the ship carrying the Copeland family and his princely belongings would sail into Halifax Harbour. As time passed with no sign or news of the *Francis*, Edward's frustration turned to concern. Had the ship gone down in a storm? Had she been captured by the French?

Edward would not likely have feared that the *Francis* had been taken by pirates. Although piracy was still a threat to shipping in some parts of the world, such as the Indian Ocean and the China Sea, it was no longer the scourge of the Atlantic it had been earlier in the century. The pirate hunters of the Royal Navy had cleared the sea lanes of such notorious predators as Edward "Blackbeard" Teach, Bartholomew "Black Bart" Roberts, and John "Calico Jack" Rackham and his lover Anne Bonny. Piracy in the Atlantic had been reduced to a minor nuisance, carried out by small-time bandits who wouldn't dare attack a ship like the *Francis* because to do so was to invite the wrath and power of the Royal Navy.

That, at least, was what Prince Edward believed. But Sir

John Wentworth had become familiar with another form of piracy during his years as governor of Nova Scotia. It was a kind of criminal activity even lower than that practised by Blackbeard, Black Bart, and Calico Jack, who had to fight for their plunder. The villains who engaged in this new form of piracy didn't need ships with cannons or crews armed with pistols and cutlasses. All they required were bad weather, a false light, and an unlucky ship. In some places they were called "blackbirds" because they were regarded as scavengers, or "mooncussers" because they cursed the light of the full moon that alerted ship captains to their traps. In Nova Scotia, they were called "wreckers."

By May of 1800, the *Francis* had still not arrived at Halifax. It was all but certain that she'd been lost. Although the ship could have fallen victim to a storm almost anywhere between England and Nova Scotia, Wentworth knew of one place where many vessels had come to grief, and believed it was worth investigating. The Royal Navy sloop the HMS *Trepassy* was about to leave Halifax on coastal patrol duty. Wentworth asked her commander, Lieutenant Jasper Scrambler, to make a stop at Sable Island to search for the *Francis*.

In the long history of transatlantic navigation, many dangerous locations on that ocean have been called the "Graveyard of the Atlantic." None has been more deserving of the grim name than Sable Island. Lying about a hundred miles off the Nova Scotia mainland, Sable Island is a giant crescent of sand, twenty miles long, and a mile across at its widest point. Sailors described it as a "snake of sand." With its highest point at less than a hundred feet and no forest cover, the island is very difficult to see from the deck of an approaching ship. In daytime, it's mostly hidden by swells and blends into the background of sea and sky. At night and in stormy or foggy weather, it is invisible.

Situated near well-travelled shipping lanes, Sable Island was a beast of prey more fearsome than the sea serpents that haunted the dreams of superstitious sailors. It devoured ships that had been blown off course in storms, ships whose captains had made navigational errors, and ships that had gotten lost in fog. Wrecked vessels and the bones of their crews would be buried under the wind-blown and surf-lain sand.

However, the waters around Sable Island have proven to be even more deadly than the island itself. Sable Island is the most prominent feature of a massive sand deposit on the North American continental shelf, and for miles in every direction are hidden ship traps: sandbars that constantly shift with the currents. A vessel that would run aground on one of those submerged hazards and was unable to get free was doomed. It would be pounded to pieces by the relentless waves or slip down into an undersea trough to be buried forever under sand and water.

For the people on a ship snared by a sandbar, the chances of survival were slim. It was almost like being stranded in a swamp in the middle of an ocean. Shipwreck survivors, huddled in tiny lifeboats, would have to fight the elements and devilish currents while navigating the maze of sand-bars to get to the island. In darkness or fog, they might not even know which way to go. Those who did manage to reach Sable Island found only a barren shore. With the exception of a lucky few who were rescued by fishermen or seal hunters, they died there.

At least fourteen ships that were wrecked on Sable Island between 1757 and 1797 had no survivors. Those were just the ones whose fates were known because searchers found evidence of the disasters. Others vanished without a trace.

From the few wrecks that left living witnesses came harrowing tales of survival. Castaways used the timbers from shattered vessels to build crude shelters and fuel fires. If they were fortunate, they had food salvaged from the wreck. Otherwise they subsisted on eggs, shellfish, and berries. If they had the necessary tools, they could catch fish or hunt seabirds and seals. A few ponds on the island provided fresh water.

But these were the bare essentials of life and did little to offset the soul-wrenching despair and loneliness of being stranded on a spit of sand in the middle of nowhere. One shipwrecked sailor was raging mad by the time a passing vessel picked him up. Seven women, the only survivors of a wrecked French ship, allegedly lived on the island for years before being found.

One of the most well-documented Sable Island shipwreck stories was that of the *Catherine*, which in 1737 sailed from Ireland for Boston with 202 men, women, and children on board. Among the passengers were two wealthy merchants who carried several thousand pounds sterling in gold and silver coins with the intention of establishing a business in the colonies. Many of their fellow travellers, expecting to settle in New England, had brought along their family "estates": gold and silver plate and jew-ellery. It was said that the *Catherine* was one of the richest ships that ever left Ireland.

The *Catherine* never reached Boston. On the night of July 17, 1737, a storm drove the ship into the maw of Sable Island. First, the *Catherine* struck a sandbar about a mile from Sable's eastern end. Then wind and currents dragged her to be smashed to pieces on the island's shore. Ninety-eight people died in the initial wreck. Three or four more drowned trying to get to the beach.

The morning after the disaster, the battered survivors built a rough shelter out of wreckage and a sail in the lee of a dune. They then buried any bodies that had been washed up by the surf. Amid the flotsam, they found a few feather mattresses which they cut up and wrapped around them-selves for warmth.

By a stroke of good luck, the shipwrecked people found the *Catherine's* longboat. It was damaged, but not badly. Fortunately, the tool chest belonging to the ship's carpen-ter was among the salvaged items. While foraging parties searched for food, sailors patched up the longboat.

Three days later, the captain, his mate, and seven other mariners pushed off for the port of Canso, about a hundred miles away. Thanks to good weather and a calm sea, the trip took them only two days. The commander of the mili-tary garrison dispatched a schooner that picked up the rest of the *Catherine's* people on July 25, 1737. The merchants' gold and silver coins and the other passengers' family trea-sures were lost and have never been found.

At various times there had been attempts to establish

permanent habitations on the island. The French had even tried to use it as the site of a penal colony. Those endeavours had all failed miserably. However, a long lasting result of human activity on the island was a herd of wild horses. Exactly how and why they got there is uncertain, but the introduction of the original domestic animals seems to have occurred about the time of the British expulsion of French settlers from Acadia in the mid-eighteenth century.

In 1789, a Nova Scotian named Jesse Lawrence who was living on Sable Island was attacked by a party of men from Massachusetts. The New Englanders destroyed his house and property and ordered him off the island. Lawrence made his living hunting seals, and he claimed to have chosen Sable Island as his base so he could be on hand to assist shipwrecked sailors. The vigilantes from Massachusetts clearly had doubts about Lawrence's altruism.

There had been an increase in the frequency of shipwrecks on Sable Island, and some of the folks in Massachusetts didn't think they were all strictly accidental. They suspected Lawrence of being a wrecker. If they'd had proof that he was definitely involved in that nefarious business, they might have done more than just run him off the island. In the newly independent United States, road agents who had been apprehended were often dragged out of jail and lynched.

Lawrence's eviction from Sable Island by the Yankees caused considerable indignation in Nova Scotia. The colonial government complained to the Massachusetts Council, which subsequently compensated Lawrence for a small percentage of his losses. After that, Jesse Lawrence's name disappears from record, so it isn't known if he really was a wrecker.

The name "wrecker" applied to two different groups of people who profited from shipwrecks. It would be more accurate to describe the first group as salvagers. Their activity was as old as navigation. When a ship was wrecked on or near the coast, timbers, spars, rigging, sails, and cargo washed ashore. Local people would help themselves to the windfall from the sea. After a shipwreck, it wasn't uncommon for families in nearby communities to have their larders filled with barrels of flour, apples, and beer that had been picked up on the beach. Shoes, clothing, household items, and other merchandise found their way onto shop-owners' shelves. A grounded and abandoned vessel would be stripped of timbers that were then used in the construction of houses and barns, in spite of a superstition that a building made from the wood of a wrecked ship was haunted by the cries of drowning sailors.

Many people in small fishing and farming communities, where life was hard and money was scarce, saw nothing wrong with salvaging goods from a misfortune that was no fault of their own. The reasoning was that if they didn't scoop up the booty, someone else would. Other people, usually those who were better off financially, looked down on it as scavenging.

Nonetheless, whenever word spread along a coastal area that a ship was in trouble, local people invariably turned out to do whatever they could to help the passengers and crew reach safety. Boats would be launched in perilous rescue operations. Half-drowned, shivering survivors would be taken into homes and offered the comforts of warm fires, hot tea, and dry blankets. Only after that would the beaches and wreck be raided for plunder.

The second group of people called wreckers were pirates of the most despicable kind. To them a shipwreck meant loot and nothing else. Rather than wait for the sea to send them a victim by chance, they would lure a ship to destruction with false lights in foggy weather and on nights when there was no moonlight. The people on a ship that fell into the trap were doomed. When the wreckers rowed out in their longboats to plunder the prize, they ignored the cries of those struggling in the water. Any poor soul who made it to dry land was murdered for the cold, practical reason that the dead tell no tales.

Isolated Sable Island was the ideal location for piratical wreckers. It had no residents with prying eyes. Its reputation as a natural ship trap ensured that no one would ever know for certain if a missing vessel had been wrecked by accident or by cruel design. When Governor Wentworth sent Lieutenant Scrambler to investigate Sable Island, he hoped that if the *Francis* had in fact been wrecked there, it had been due to natural circumstances because that meant there could be survivors. If it had been the work of wreckers, there would be none.

The *Trepassy* reached Sable Island on May 13, 1800. Search parties found no survivors and no trace of the *Francis*. As the sloop carefully picked its way along the north shore, the lookout spotted a schooner riding at anchor. At the Royal Navy vessel's approach, the schooner's crew suddenly began hauling up the anchor and setting their sails as though preparing to flee. But the swift *Trepassy* came alongside the schooner before she could get under way. The crew had no choice but to allow Lieutenant Scrambler and an armed party to come aboard.

The schooner was the *Dolphin*, out of Barrington, Nova Scotia. The captain was a man named Reynolds. Scrambler found the hold full of seal skins, seal oil, and fish. He also found evidence of the *Francis*. The lieutenant wrote in his report:

"She had several trunks very much damaged on board, and appeared to have been washed on shore. One trunk was directed to His Royal Highness Prince Edward, No. 2, another trunk directed to Captain Sterling of the 7th Regiment of Foot, both empty. Also a trunk containing two greatcoats, the livery worn by the servants of His Royal Highness."

Captain Reynolds told Scrambler that the items had been found by two of his men, Coleman Crowell and Ziba Hunt. On Scrambler's order, the two were brought to him for questioning. Explaining to a Royal Navy officer how they came to be in possession of the prince's property, which had last been seen on a now-missing ship, must have been an unnerving experience.

Crowell and Hunt said that Reynolds had left them on Sable Island in the spring of 1799 to hunt seals and, as they put it, "look for wrecks." Exactly what they meant by that wasn't clear, though it might have referred to scavenging. Sable's shifting sands often revealed the remains of long-lost vessels.

Reynolds was supposed to pick the men up in September,

but had been prevented from doing so by foul weather. Crowell and Hunt were stranded for the winter. They survived on berries, fish, and horsemeat.

Then one day in late December, they saw the *Francis* off the island's northeast bar. A storm was raging, and the ship was clearly in trouble, fighting wind and currents. A day later, the ship was gone. The two men believed that the sandbars and the sea had swallowed her.

Soon after, wreckage from the *Francis* washed ashore. Crowell and Hunt found barrels of hardtack, cases of liquor, and crates packed with British Army red coats, soldiers' caps, and the silk hosiery worn by officers. Scattered among the debris on the beach were several bodies. One was that of a woman who was wearing a very expensive ring. Crowell and Hunt said they tried to remove the ring, but the finger was too swollen from many hours in the water. They claimed that when they buried the bodies, they put the woman in the ground with the ring still on her finger. Blowing sand soon obliterated all signs of the graves.

There had been only three women on the *Francis*: Dr. Copeland's wife and two servants. Since servants didn't own costly jewellery, Lieutenant Scrambler deduced that Crowell and Hunt had found Mrs. Copeland's body. He had doubts about much of their story.

Captain Reynolds admitted that when he had finally been able to pick up the two men earlier that spring, he had loaded the salvage from the *Francis* aboard the *Dolphin* but didn't report it. He sold the whole lot in Barrington. Townsmen were soon wearing British Army red coats and silk hosiery to local social events. Prince Edward was very displeased when he learned of this. One day he met Reynolds on a Halifax street and told him, "Your conduct, Sir, might do very well for Americans, but it is certainly not suitable for British subjects."

Reynold's failure to report the shipwreck threw a cloud of suspicion over the whole story, especially since he had tried to make a run for it when he saw the *Trepassy* bearing down on him. Would two poor sealers really have buried a valuable ring just because they couldn't pull it off the finger of its dead owner? Was the demise of the *Francis* entirely accidental? Where was the rest of Prince Edward's costly equipage?

The wreck of the *Francis* increased Sable Island's reputation as a wrecker's lair. The mystery surrounding the tragedy spawned many stories, most of them focused on Mrs. Copeland and her ring. The scenario common to all of them has the wreckers cutting off her finger to get the ring. In some accounts, it is done while she is still alive.

According to one story, Prince Edward sent a Royal Navy captain named Torrens to Sable Island to conduct a further investigation into the wreck of the *Francis.* Torrens had a chilling encounter with the ghost of Mrs. Copeland. She said she had been murdered for her ring and couldn't rest until it had been found. Torrens eventually traced the ring to a Halifax jewellery shop, where the wrecker who had stolen it placed it for sale on consignment.

Another story presented Mrs. Copeland as a former lady-in-waiting to Marie Antoinette, the ill-starred queen of France. During the chaos of the French Revolution, she had escaped to England, where she met and married

Dr. Copeland. Precious stones from the French crown jewels were allegedly sewn into the hems of her petticoats — which were lost with the *Francis*.

Because of the *Francis* disaster, the colonial government made it illegal for anyone to reside on Sable Island without a licence and began regular visits by official inspectors. New regulations were also instituted to protect shipwrecked property. Governor Wentworth was instrumental in the establishment of a permanent life-saving station on the island.

The story of the French jewels in Mrs. Copeland's petticoats was a fabrication, like many of the Sable Island treasure tales. But Prince Edward's valuable personal property was real. If wreckers had carried it off, some of the items would likely have turned up somewhere. But there have been no reports of that happening. No doubt, the prince's treasure still lies in the wreck of the *Francis*, hidden by sand and sea in the Graveyard of the Atlantic.

3

John Paul Radelmüller: From Halifax Servant to Toronto Ghost

John Paul Radelmüller's name might have been lost to historical record had it not been for a letter in his own handwriting found in the archives of the Vaughan, Ontario, public library. The letter, addressed to the Lieutenant Governor of Upper Canada, is an autobiographical account of Radelmüller's years of service with the British Royal Family. It traces the fateful journey that took a humble man from royal residences in England, to the governor's mansion in Halifax, and finally to a lighthouse on Lake Ontario that is said to be haunted by his ghost.

Radelmüller was born around 1763 in Anspach, Germany. That was the hometown of Queen Caroline, the wife of England's King George II. Strong connections between the English monarchy and Germany had existed since 1714, when Queen Anne died without an heir, and her cousin, George Louis Guelph of Hanover, became King George I. George I and his descendants often brought Germans into their households as staff. Radelmüller must have come from a respectable and well-connected family. He wrote, "In the year 1782 ... I had the Honor to become a Servant to H.R. [His Royal] Highness the Duke of Gloucester in the Character as Chamber Hussar in which Service and Station I remained until 1798."

In the sixteen years that he served Prince William Henry, Duke of Gloucester and Edinburgh, King George III's brother, Radelmüller would have witnessed many of the scandals and foibles of a dysfunctional royal family. George III was slipping into madness. His heir, George, the Prince of Wales, was nicknamed "The Contagion" because of his selfish, boorish behaviour. The Duke of Gloucester was banned from court because he had secretly married a woman without asking the king's permission. The duke's son, William Frederick, was described as "boring, dense, and conceited." His royal relatives called him "the imbecile cousin." To the British public he was "Silly Billy."

Spoiled royals must have made life hell for servants like Radelmüller. But the Duke of Gloucester liked to travel, and he took Radelmüller with him on his tours. That experience would prove valuable to him.

In 1798, perhaps having had enough of life as a royal servant, Radelmüller went back to Anspach. He wrote that he wanted to take up "farmering" and get reacquainted with his family. However, war and revolution were rolling across Europe. "As I knowed that I was willcome [sic] again where I came from, after a few months stay I turn'd a gain [sic] to Old England. As it hapened [sic] then H.R. Highness the Duke of Kent came home from America. I had the Honor soon after his arrival to engage myself with Him as porter."

The Duke of Kent was Prince Edward Augustus, fourth son of King George III, and in whose honour Prince Edward Island was named. The king didn't like Edward, possibly because his birth coincided with the sudden death of Edward the Duke of York, his favourite brother.

George III packed young Edward Augustus off to military school in Germany. Then, to keep the prince out of his sight, he assigned him to military commands at various outposts of the empire. Edward saw duty in Gibraltar, the West Indies, Quebec, and Nova Scotia. In Halifax, Edward had overseen improvements to the city's defences, including Citadel Hill. He also earned a reputation as a harsh commander. When Radelmüller joined Edward's household staff, the prince was on a visit home to recover from an injury he'd suffered in a riding accident in Nova Scotia. Anxious to get Edward out of England again, George III made him commander-in-chief of all armed forces in British North America and ordered him back to Halifax.

As Edward's porter, Radelmüller would be sailing for the colonies. "Since I was an old travelor [sic] I got the charge of the packages." That meant he was in charge of overseeing the packing and preparation for sea transport of Edward's wardrobe, furniture, military equipage, and everything else a prince needed, from silverware to toilet chair. It was an enormous responsibility.

As a member of Edward's household "family," Radelmüller witnessed one of the most scandalous romantic affairs of the time. Edward had fallen in love with

Alphonsine-Thérèse-Bernardine-Julie Montgenêt de St. Laurent. Beautiful, clever, and known for her wit, Julie came from a respectable French family. However, Edward couldn't marry her because she was not of royal blood and she was already the wife of a French army officer. Nonetheless, Julie was Edward's wife in all but name, and he took her with him wherever he went, which infuriated the king. Julie managed Edward's household, so would have become well acquainted with Radelmüller.

Edward, Julie, and a retinue of servants that included Radelmüller embarked from Portsmouth aboard the frigate *Arethusa* on July 25, 1799. They docked in Halifax forty-three days later with cannon salutes and church bells announcing their arrival. Sir John Wentworth, the governor of Nova Scotia, greeted them. The prince and the governor had struck up a cordial relationship during Edward's previous sojourn in Halifax. Wentworth provided Edward and Julie with a house called the Lodge on Bedford Basin.

Radelmüller and the other servants at the Lodge would have been kept busy. As a representative of the royal family, Edward was a central figure of social activity. He was expected to be at formal and festive events and to host dinners and other gatherings at his residence. Radelmüller would have seen that some of the narrow attitudes of high society were alive and well in the colonial capital. There were those among Halifax's tiny social elite who disapproved of Edward's relationship with his "French lady," and Julie was not invited to their homes.

Their snootiness was made all the more absurd by the fact that Sir John Wentworth and his wife Frances were long-standing objects of gossip and innuendo. They had what today would be called an open marriage. Each carried on extramarital affairs of which the other was fully aware. Lady Wentworth had even had a fling with Edward's older brother, Prince William Henry (later King William IV), when he visited Halifax as a Royal Navy officer.

Sir John and Frances thought their marital arrangement was civilized. To most Haligonians, it was shocking. But that didn't stop the city's most prominent residents from turning a blind eye when seeking the governor's favour. To Radelmüller, who had observed the royal family's antics for almost twenty years, the sins of the Wentworths were probably not at all surprising.

Radelmüller took advantage of his days off to explore the country beyond Halifax. He still had ideas about "farmering," and liked what he saw of Nova Scotia. Edward had intended to visit Newfoundland and Quebec, but after just a year in Halifax he fell ill and decided to go back to England. Radelmüller wanted to stay. Edward made an offer that seemed like a godsend. Radelmüller wrote:

"He inquired if there were any in His Family that should be desirous to Settle in this Country, and ask'd me if I am one of them. I answered in the affirmative. His R.H.s well knows that I wished to have Land. He offered me His Assistance for some without my asking for any, and were [where] I would like to have it if there should be any vacant. I thank'd him for the kind offer and I soon found out some vacant Land not far from Halifax ones [once] designed for an Officer but hapen'd [sic] to die before he locate it, by this it remained vacant, which said

Land consisted of a Thousand acres more or less. I took the Liberty to inform H.R.H. of the aforesaid Land. He said as I had served so many years in the Family faithfully he thinks me worthy of it, and will help me to it."

Edward also said he would get Radelmüller a suitable job in the colonial government. Radelmüller said the prince believed "it would be a pity to be hid in the Bush." The servant was overjoyed.

Then came a stroke of bad luck. Just before Edward and Julie were due to embark, the man they had hired as Radelmüller's replacement got sick. Edward said that they couldn't do without the services of a good porter and asked Radelmüller to return to England with them. He promised to pay for Radelmüller's return passage to Nova Scotia. Disappointed, but ever the loyal servant, Radelmüller was aboard the HMS *Assistance* when she sailed from Halifax on August 4, 1800.

Back in London, Edward set Julie up in a house in Knightsbridge, while he discreetly resided at Kensington Palace. Both were ill for months, blaming the Nova Scotia climate. Radelmüller felt duty bound to stay in London and be of service to them until their health improved. A year passed before Edward kept his promise to pay for Radelmüller's passage back to Nova Scotia.

The love affair of Prince Edward and Julie didn't have a fairy tale ending. In order to produce a legitimate heir to the British throne, he had to give her up (with a generous financial settlement) so he could marry a German princess. The sole child from that marriage became Queen Victoria.

Back in Halifax in 1801, Radelmüller was disappointed

to learn that the government job Edward had promised him was no longer available. However, Governor Wentworth offered him the position of head steward in his household. Radelmüller readily accepted. No doubt, Sir John enjoyed the prestige of having a steward who had been in the service of royalty.

Radelmüller worked for the Wentworths for two years. "I found His Excellency a very just and good Governor," he wrote. But Radelmüller was approaching forty, "getting in years" as he put it, and wanted to "redire [sic] a little before I die in my own way."

Radelmüller inspected the thousand-acre property he'd been promised but decided that it wasn't very well suited for "farmering." He'd heard that much better land was available in Upper Canada. He decided he wanted to go there.

Like most Europeans, Radelmüller had little understanding of the geography of North America. He didn't realize that York (Toronto) was almost as far by ship from Halifax as Halifax was from England. And he came to a disheartening discovery that he didn't know the "just and good Governor" as well as he had thought.

Radelmüller told Wentworth of his wish to go to Upper Canada, and gave him six months' notice. That allowed him plenty of time to make his travel arrangements and gave Wentworth more than enough time to find a new steward. Wentworth said he was sorry to see Radelmüller go, but would provide him with letters of recommendation and character. Such documents were essential for a man, especially a foreigner, going to a new place where he knew nobody. Radelmüller was grateful for the governor's understanding and promise of help.

On November 23, 1803, Radelmüller stood on the Halifax dock. His belongings were on a ship whose captain was impatiently calling for him to get aboard or the ship would sail without him. Radelmüller was anxiously waiting for Wentworth to come and see him off and give him those all-important papers. Wentworth finally showed up, but he didn't have the papers.

Wentworth pleaded with Radelmüller to stay with him for at least another winter. He argued that servants of such quality were almost impossible to find in Halifax. But Radelmüller's mind was made up and the captain was shouting a final warning.

Wentworth reluctantly promised that he would mail Radelmüller's documents to the Lieutenant Governor of Upper Canada. He said they would go with the next fast packet and would probably be waiting for him by the time he reached York. Disappointed again, Radelmüller hurried aboard his ship before the sailors hauled in the gangplank. "I took the Resolution to set off in the Name of God and a fair Wind for Upper Canada without the least Recommendation or Character, except a Clear Conscience and a Burs ful [purse full] of money, and I am in Expectation to get better used."

Radelmüller's journey by way of the Gulf of St. Lawrence, the St. Lawrence River, and Lake Ontario took five weeks. Whenever he saw the distant sail of a small, speedy packet bypassing his slower transport vessel, he must have wondered if it was carrying his documents. He finally docked at York on January 1, 1804.

Radelmüller's first sight of York must have come as a shock to him. He had lived most of his adult life in London, the largest urban centre in Europe. York, which had been founded by John Graves Simcoe barely a decade earlier, was a tiny community of wooden buildings and a few muddy streets perched on the shore of Lake Ontario. Beyond was a howling wilderness. Compared to York, even colonial Halifax was a bustling metropolis.

Radelmüller went straight to Lieutenant Governor of Upper Canada Peter Hunter to introduce himself and ask for the documents he was certain would be waiting for him. But they weren't there. It took seven more months, and Hunter's request on Radelmüller's behalf, before Governor Wentworth finally kept his promise and sent the papers.

Meanwhile, Radelmüller was determined to make the best of the situation. Rugged York didn't seem to be the most favourable location for a former royal house servant, but he was resourceful. He taught English to a community of German-speaking immigrants, the Pennsylvania Dutch, who had settled in Markham Township. Hunter was impressed with Radelmüller's letters of recommendation and character, and hired him as the colonial government's official German interpreter. Radelmüller had authority equal to that of a justice of the peace when dealing with immigrants' legal affairs.

Radelmüller had found employment and acceptance in Upper Canada, but he still dreamed of having his own land. The country around York had already been taken up by

settlers who were hacking farms out of the forest. Radelmüller thought his connections with Prince Edward and
Governor Wentworth might make him eligible for one of
the Crown Reserve lots, properties that for various reasons
were not open for settlement.

To support his request, Radelmüller wrote the letter to
Hunter in which he told his life story, drawing the lieutenant governor's attention to his years of service with the
royal family and Wentworth. However, Crown land was
untouchable, and Hunter was obliged to turn him down.
Four years later, Radelmüller tried again with Hunter's replacement, Major Francis Gore, with the same result.

Nonetheless, Radelmüller's sterling credentials and good
standing in the community gained him a plum government job. In July 1809, Gore made him the keeper of the
new lighthouse that had been erected on Toronto Island's
Gibraltar Point. It was the first permanent lighthouse on
the Great Lakes. It was a position of great responsibility
that called for a reliable, competent man.

Radelmüller moved into a cabin beside the lighthouse.
In 1810, he married Magdalena Burkholder, with whom
he had a daughter. The family lived quietly on the island,
which at that time was somewhat isolated from York.

During the War of 1812, American invaders captured
and burned York. The only important building they didn't
destroy was the lighthouse. They were afraid to approach
the stone tower out of fear that the British had mined it.

Radelmüller's end is shrouded in mystery. On January
14, 1815, the *York Gazette* reported, "Died on the evening
of the 2nd of January, J.P. Radan Muller [sic], keeper of

the lighthouse on Gibraltar Point. From the circumstances there is moral proof of his having been murdered."

Allegedly, intoxicated soldiers from Fort York went out to the lighthouse to buy some of Radelmüller's home-brewed German beer. They quarreled with him and killed him in a drunken rage. Two soldiers were arrested but acquitted. The problem for the Crown Prosecutor was that there was no body. John Paul Radelmüller had vanished from the face of the earth.

A story circulated that the murderous soldiers had dismembered Radelmüller's body and buried the parts all over the island. Soon there were tales about Radelmüller's ghost wandering the island at night, searching for his lost bones. The lighthouse became a centre of supernatural lore, supposedly haunted by the keeper's ghost.

John Paul Radelmüller is best known as the ghost of the Gibraltar Point lighthouse, which today is one of Toronto's most famous haunted sites. But the brief inscription on the bronze historic plaque makes no mention of the story that reaches back to Nova Scotia and to England where the faithful German servant walked in the shadow of royalty.

4

Coghlan's Coffin: Prince Edward Island's Grave Mystery

"The memory of an actor like Charles Coghlan will not soon vanish." This statement was not part of an obituary, but praise from Toronto theatre critic Kenyon West in the *Toronto Globe* on April 30, 1898. West had just seen the actor, whom theatre historians would call "the John Barrymore of his day," give an electrifying performance in *The Royal Box*, a play Coghlan had adapted from Alexander Dumas' drama, *Kean*. However, it was not Coghlan's fame as an actor, but a strange legend that would keep his name alive in posterity and tie it to Prince Edward Island.

Charles Francis Coghlan was not, as some stories claim, born on Prince Edward Island. He was born in Paris in 1841 or 1842. His father, Francis, was a publisher from Dublin whose literary associates included Charles Dickens. His mother, Amie Marie, was from the Island of Jersey.

Coghlan's parents wanted him to become a lawyer and sent him to schools in France and England. But while still a teenager, Coghlan was drawn to the glittering excitement of the theatre, an attraction he shared with his sister Rose. They often attended opening night at the Théâtre-Français in Paris.

In 1859, Coghlan began his stage career playing minor roles for a touring English theatrical troupe. He learned his craft in cities like Birmingham and Dublin. By the mid-1860s he was performing in London, winning critical praise. Rose was also a rising star in British theatre.

By the early 1870s, Coghlan was among the most celebrated actors in London's prestigious West End theatre district. He played lead roles in contemporary dramas and comedies and was a brilliant Shakespearean actor. He enthralled audiences whether he played a hero or a villain.

Coghlan mastered an element of acting called "repressed force." One critic wrote of him years later, "In all Coghlan's acting there was a pleasing propriety of art. The thought preceded the speech. The gesture came before the word. All that was said and done seemed to be said and done for the first time."

Coghlan's name was box-office gold. He performed in the works of some of the greatest playwrights of his time, including George Bernard Shaw and Oscar Wilde. He was an accomplished author himself, writing original plays and adapting the works of others to the stage. His play *Lady Barter* starred Lily Langtry, "The Jersey Lily," one of the greatest actresses of the day. When Coghlan wasn't performing in front of an audience, he was behind the scenes directing.

Coghlan was a superstar long before the word was coined. However, in spite of his great success, Coghlan never stayed with any theatrical company for long. He moved from one to another like a wandering thespian from an earlier age. Fellow actors said he sometimes spoke of living under a curse.

Coghlan lived in a time of great change. Science and new concepts of reason challenged traditional Victorian beliefs. But old superstitions didn't vanish overnight. People still believed there were mysterious ways in which their futures could be revealed by means of crystal balls, tarot cards, tea leaves, and the lines in the palms of their hands. Coghlan allegedly visited a woman who presented herself as a "gypsy fortune teller." She made a disturbing prediction. She told Coghlan he would die suddenly at the peak of his success and his body would not rest peacefully in its grave.

In his private life, Coghlan moved in the highest social circles. He was an honoured guest in London's finest homes and dined with the rich and famous in the city's most exclusive clubs and restaurants. Coghlan was a friend of the Prince of Wales (the future King Edward VII) and was the first actor ever invited to give a personal performance for the prince and his family at the royal residence in Sandringham.

In 1876, a leading American producer, Augustin Daly, brought Coghlan to New York to perform on Broadway. The actor Daly hailed as "a leading man of distinction and personal charm" was an instant sensation. His performances repeatedly brought American audiences to their feet. Coghlan was soon the most highly paid actor in the United States.

Coghlan spent most of the remainder of his career in

North America, performing in one hit show after another. He and Lily Langtry were outstanding when they appeared together in *Macbeth* and *Antony and Cleopatra*. But to many who knew him, Coghlan seemed to be haunted by the spectre of a cruel fate he couldn't escape. He also became the central player in a scandal.

Coghlan was in his early fifties in 1893 when he married a beautiful young sculptress named Kuhne Beveridge. The fact that Kuhne was only nineteen years old was enough to set tongues wagging. That she was the granddaughter of John Lourie Beveridge, ex-congressman, former governor of Illinois, and a Civil War hero, made the gossip even juicier. But what really shocked the American public was the revelation that for twenty-five years, Coghlan had been in a common-law relationship with English actress Louisa Elizabeth Thorn. They had a daughter named Gertrude, an aspiring actress who was only a year older than Kuhne.

In that era, such scandals outraged the public and destroyed reputations and careers. The unsympathetic press gleefully dubbed Kuhne "Mrs. Coghlan Number Two." Humiliated, Kuhne ended her relationship with Coghlan and had the marriage annulled. Coghlan returned to the forgiving Louisa, fortunate not to have been investigated on suspicion of bigamy. The ripple effect of that scandal would continue for years, causing public embarrassment for the Coghlan family.

Coghlan spent much of his professional life on the road, performing all over North America. At some point in his travels, he visited Prince Edward Island. Coghlan was enchanted by the island's natural beauty and its romantic lore. He especially loved Fortune Bay, where the legendary Captain William Kidd had supposedly buried pirate treasure. The community had a popular actors' colony that Coghlan became involved with, so he bought a house there. In keeping with the Coghlan saga, the house had a colourful history.

In September 1819, a flint-hearted landlord named Edward Abell rented it to Patrick Pearce, a young farmer. Abell and Pearce quarrelled over money, and in a fit of anger, the farmer stabbed the landlord to death with a bayonet. The law placed a reward of £20 on Pearce's head, and he went into hiding.

Twenty pounds was a lot of money, but Pearce's neighbours wouldn't betray the man who had killed the overbearing Abell. For months, they hid Pearce in their cellars and told nosey constables they hadn't seen him. Allegedly, a farmer named Joseph Brown had a tunnel running from his house to a nearby creek in case Pearce had to make a hasty escape. When spring arrived, Pearce disguised himself in women's clothing, rowed out to a visiting American ship, and was never seen on the island again.

It didn't bother Coghlan that the house was associated with a murder. He probably enjoyed the tales about it being haunted by Abell's ghost. He found it a relaxing retreat to escape the stresses of celebrity and the occasional scandal. He wrote plays there, including *The Royal Box*, in which he shared the stage with Gertrude.

The Royal Box was a smash hit in New York. Critics poured out their admiration for Coghlan and his work as an actor, writer, and director. One wrote, "He is a stirling (sic) artist, finished, polished, careful of every detail, working up to the finest effects by the simplest, most natural means."

Coghlan was at the pinnacle of his career. He decided to take his incredibly successful play on the road, stopping at cities all over the United States and Canada. *The Royal Box* was performed in Toronto, where the *Globe* informed theatre patrons, "You are to be congratulated on having the opportunity to see Mr. Coghlan and his admirable company." However, it was during this long tour that disaster struck.

On October 28, 1899, Coghlan's company performed *The Royal Box* in Houston, Texas. It would be his final appearance on stage. The company moved on to Galveston, where Coghlan was suddenly stricken with gastritis. After a few weeks of illness, he died on November 27, 1899. Part of the "gypsy curse" had seemingly come true. The question remains as to whether or not Coghlan had succumbed to his ailment because he believed he was doomed.

Coghlan had told Rose that in the event of his death, he wanted his remains to be cremated. But his sister was in Canada when he died. Gertrude, who had been touring with her father, was grief-stricken and unsure of what to do. At that time, many people considered cremation of the dead unchristian.

Coghlan's body was placed in a metal coffin and interred in a local seaside cemetery. Due to the area's vulnerability to flooding, the dead in the cemetery were not buried six feet down, but enclosed in above-ground vaults. The arrangement was meant to be temporary, until a decision could be made as to his final resting place.

At first, family members said the body would be transported to Prince Edward Island for burial at Fortune Bay, the place to which they said he would have retired. But Rose must have decided that her brother's own wish should be respected, because soon after, it was announced in the press that Coghlan's remains would be sent to New York for cremation. Months passed, however, and the body remained in the Galveston cemetery. Within a year of Coghlan's death, the second part of the gypsy curse was fulfilled.

On September 9, 1900, the Texas Gulf Coast was savaged by one of the worst hurricanes in recorded history. Galveston was hit especially hard. A massive storm surge inundated coastal areas, and the cemetery in which Coghlan had been interred was swept out to sea.

The bones of many of the deceased were lost forever in the Gulf of Mexico, but from time to time, caskets and human remains were found washed up along the Texas coast. The New York Actors' Club offered a reward for anyone who found Coghlan's coffin. In 1907, a group of hunters found a coffin that was believed to be his, partly submerged in a swamp about nine miles from Galveston. The story of Coghlan's coffin might have ended there had it not been for Robert Ripley, creator of *Ripley's Believe It or Not!*

By the 1920s, Charles Coghlan had been largely forgotten. Thomas Edison's motion picture camera had brought the world a new form of entertainment and a new galaxy of "stars." Live theatre still had its loyal followers, but crowds were going to the movies to see Mary Pickford and

Charlie Chaplin.

Then on September 15, 1927, an incredible story appeared in Ripley's syndicated feature:

> *Believe It or Not Charles Coghlan Comes Home! He died in 1899 and was buried in Galveston. When the tragic flood came his coffin was washed out to sea and the Gulf Stream carried him around Florida and up the coast to Prince Edward Island — 2,000 miles distant — where he was born.*

The story wasn't entirely Ripley's invention. His sources were the memoirs of the actor Sir Johnston Forbes-Robertson, *A Player Under Three Reigns*, and Lily Langtry's autobiography, *The Days I Knew.* Langtry devoted a few paragraphs to Coghlan, in which she described him as being "brainy but temperamental." She wrote about Coghlan's fear of the gypsy curse, his death and burial in Galveston, and the storm that washed away the cemetery. She said nothing about the coffin floating to Prince Edward Island. However, Forbes-Robertson's book, published two years before the Ripley feature appeared, did include the story of the coffin's amazing voyage.

The origin of the legend Forbes-Robertson related is unknown, but one version says that ten years after the Galveston hurricane, fishermen spotted an oblong box in the water off Fortune Bay. Not until they hauled it ashore did they realize that it was a coffin. An engraved metal plate bore the name Charles F. Coghlan. The fishermen respectfully buried the coffin at a site overlooking Fortune Bay.

British poet and dramatist W.H. Auden came across the story (though he said he couldn't remember where) and gave Coghlan a touch of literary immortality when he and co-author Christopher Isherwood included these lines in a chorus of their play, *The Dog Beneath the Skin* (1935):

And death moves in to take his inner luck
Lands on the beaches of his love, like Coghlan's coffin.

Neither the Ripley feature nor the legend identifies the exact location of Coghlan's grave at Fortune Bay. Gertrude insisted that there was no truth to the story. She didn't accept that the coffin discovered in the Texas swamp was Coghlan's because she had spent years and thousands of dollars searching for her father's remains, but had found nothing.

A new twist was added to the tale with the death of another famous actor. Charles Flockton was almost as renowned as Coghlan. Oscar Wilde considered him one of the best American actors of the time. Flockton was also drawn by the beauty of Prince Edward Island, and he and his comedy company became regular visitors. In 1894, Flockton bought property at Fortune Bay. He might have met Coghlan there. Later, Flockton even lived in Coghlan's old house. He expressed his wish to be buried at Fortune Bay.

Flockton died in 1904, and his burial became linked to the mystery of Coghlan's coffin. One story says that Flockton's body was cremated and his ashes buried at Fortune Bay. His friends marked the site with a monument topped by a sundial with an inscription: "In memory of a faithful friend and loyal servant. The creeping shadow marks another hour of absence."

To most people, the word "absence" referred to the fact that Flockton had passed from this world. But it sparked a rumour that Flockton's remains were absent from the grave. A story arose that challenged the Coghlan legend. In this tale, Flockton died in San Francisco and was buried in a seaside cemetery. In the disastrous San Francisco earthquake of 1906, the cemetery fell into the sea. Flockton's coffin floated all the way from California to Prince Edward Island, and it was the one the fishermen found and buried.

The story of Coghlan's coffin is the product of fanciful imagination. But it has given the long dead actor a niche in the lore of Atlantic Canada. Coghlan continues to play a part in an unusual drama more than a century after he made his last curtain call.

PART II

SMUGGLERS AND GANGSTERS

5

Captain Jack Randell: The Sinking of the *I'm Alone*

In the summer of 1928, a man representing a group of Montreal businessmen visited Captain Jack Randell at his home in Port Rexton, Newfoundland. He offered Randell command of a schooner the group had purchased for rum-running. There were good reasons that the Montrealers wanted Randell. He was one of the most highly respected sea captains in Newfoundland, and he already had plenty of experience running bootleg liquor into the United States.

Born on January 1, 1879, Randell had the blood of adventurers in his veins. His ancestors had sailed with Francis Drake, Martin Frobisher, and Lord Nelson. His great-great-grandfather, Captain John Randell, had arrived in Newfoundland in 1715 aboard a Royal Navy warship and made the colony his home.

The sea had been Randell's school. He made his first trip to the Labrador fishing grounds at the age of twelve. At sixteen, he sailed to Brazil as a crewman on a square-rigged brigantine. Randell served with distinction in the Boer War and the Great War and was personally decorated by King George V. In peacetime, he commanded ships on expeditions into the Arctic. He was equally at home under sail or on the bridge of a steamship.

Attracted by big money, Randell had first ventured into the rum-running business in 1922. He operated from a fleet of offshore "mother ships" called Rum Row and smuggled liquor directly into major ports such as New York City. He quickly gained a reputation as a reliable and fearless rum-runner.

On one occasion, when a gang of hoodlums tried to hijack his cargo, Randell used a boat's tiller as a cudgel and put to flight any thugs he didn't knock out. In another incident, the boat in which Randell and an American bootlegger were ferrying cargo ashore was swamped by a heavy swell. While the American cried in terror, Randell bellowed, "Hell! Kids swim in this kind of a sea in Newfoundland!"

But smuggling held other dangers. Crooked New York cops shook Randell down for money. City-bred bootleggers who didn't know a thing about the sea expected him to sail untrustworthy vessels in the foulest of weather. Worst of all, they swindled him out of money. In 1927, Randell quit.

Randell's first response to the visitor from Montreal was a flat refusal. He had no desire to resume taking big risks only to be cheated. He said he'd had his fill of gangsters, con men, and harbour scum.

The visitor explained that things had changed. Big

syndicates had driven out most of the small-time hoodlums. The Montrealers Randell would be working for had developed an efficient, professional, foolproof system. They would handle the financial transactions and had all the legal points covered. Randell's job was to deliver cargo to a specific location and to have no contact with independent operators. As long as he kept out of American territorial waters, he had no reason to be concerned about the United States Coast Guard. He would be well paid in whatever manner he chose.

Randell was impressed with the high level of organization. But he had one important question: "What schooner?"

The man replied, "Her name is the *I'm Alone*."

Randell knew the ship. The *I'm Alone* was a two-masted schooner from Nova Scotia equipped with twin 110 horsepower diesel engines. She was a sleek, fast vessel that handled well in heavy seas. But one thing made Randell uneasy. For years, a Boston-based smuggler had used the *I'm Alone* as a rum-runner. The schooner was on the Coast Guard blacklist.

When Randell expressed concern, his visitor told him the Boston bootlegger was in prison. The *I'm Alone* had changed hands twice since his arrest, and was registered to legitimate Canadian owners. The Coast Guard had no legal reason to stop her. Randell finally agreed to take command of the *I'm Alone*.

Randell sailed the *I'm Alone* out of Halifax on November 4, 1928. At Saint-Pierre, he picked up a cargo of liquor. He was given sealed orders that he was not to open until he was in the Gulf of Mexico.

They directed him to a location off the coast of Louisiana, where he was to await his contact.

Randell followed his orders to the letter. He arrived at the location, but saw no sign of a launch from shore. Instead, the Coast Guard cutter *Walcott* steamed into view. Randell had no reason to flee because he was outside the three-mile limit. But his contact wouldn't approach with the Coast Guard hanging around.

The *I'm Alone* sailed away and the *Walcott* followed. Several times, the cutter came alongside the schooner, but the commander didn't hail Randell. This continued for twenty-four hours as the *I'm Alone* took a southerly course across the Gulf.

By the second night, Randell had had enough of the *Walcott*. He doused his lights. In the darkness, he took advantage of the *I'm Alone's* speed to outmaneuver the cutter and slip away into the pitch black night.

The *I'm Alone* sailed to Belize City, the capital of British Honduras (now Belize). Randell cabled his employers in Montreal, explained what had happened and requested further instructions. A day later he received orders sending him to a new rendezvous.

This time, all went smoothly

Belize City was Randell's port of supply. He made six trips to locations off Louisiana and Texas and didn't see a single Coast Guard cutter. Randell was on his seventh run, when just before dark, he saw the cutter *Dexter* racing toward him. Randell knew from scuttlebutt that travelled the rum-runner's grapevine that the *Dexter's* skipper, Warrant Officer Alfred W. Powell, had a reputation for being "Hard

Boiled." He was tenacious once he had a suspected smuggler in his sights.

The cutter circled the *I'm Alone*, but Powell didn't hail Randell. He just stayed close, and after darkness fell, trained his search light on the schooner from time to time.

Once again, Randell had to draw the Coast Guard away from his pickup point. After midnight, he attempted the same ruse he had used to shake the *Walcott*. It didn't work. Quite likely the *Walcott's* commander had reported how the *I'm Alone* had given him the slip.

The *Dexter* followed the *I'm Alone* for two days and nights. Every trick Randell tried failed to rid him of the pesky cutter. There was no communication between the two skippers. Every so often, the cutter would race up alongside the schooner as though Powell wanted to show Randell that making a run for it would be futile.

Late on the third day, a strong wind made the sea choppy. Randell saw that the cutter had to yaw back and forth to maintain course. She rose and fell on the swells, causing the propellers to spin uselessly when they were out of the water.

The more streamlined schooner with a deeper draft had no such problems. Randell held back on the *I'm Alone's* speed and bided his time. Several hours after nightfall, he ordered all lights out and full speed ahead. The *I'm Alone* shot straight into the wind and the darkness, leaving the *Dexter* in her wake. Four days later, Randell made his delivery and then headed for Belize City.

Randell's crewmen laughed over the trick their captain had pulled on the Coast Guard. The fact that the wily Newfoundlander's victim had been "hard-boiled" Powell made it all the better. Soon every sailor in Belize City heard the story.

The *I'm Alone* was in need of an overhaul, so Randell and his men enjoyed a few weeks of rest and relaxation. Meanwhile, the tale of the schooner's escape from the *Dexter* spread to ports all around the Gulf. Eventually, Randell learned that Powell himself had heard the story and was furious. He was a veteran of the Great War who had served aboard United States Navy submarine chasers, and it wounded his pride to be outfoxed by a rum-runner.

One sailor told Randell that he had personally said to Powell, "Smart as you think you are, that old skipper of the *I'm Alone* will outwit you every time."

Powell had allegedly replied, "I'll make you a bet, any amount you want to name, that the next time I meet up with that old son-of-a-bitch, I'll get him."

Randell was advised to be careful because Powell didn't make idle threats.

But Jack Randell had heard threats before. He was brimming with self-confidence, and he had a sturdy, dependable ship. He also commanded a first-class crew. John Williams, a fellow Newfoundlander, was mate. The bosun was Leon Maingoy, a Frenchman who had received the Croix de Guerre during the Great War. Chesley Hobbs, another Newfoundlander, was chief engineer. The assistant engineer was a Dane named Jens Jensen. The rest of the ship's company was made up of Edouard Fouchard of Miquelon, James Barrett of Montreal, and Eddie Young and William Wordsworth, both from Belize. They were all men with whom Randell shared a mutual trust.

When the *I'm Alone*'s overhaul was completed, Randell had her loaded with 3,100 cases of liquor. The value of the ship and cargo was more than $100,000. The night before departure, Randell opened a bottle so he and his men could toast good fortune. It was the last time the *I'm Alone* hosted a night of good cheer.

Randell's orders were to sail to a location south of the Trinity Shoals, about sixty miles off the Louisiana coast. Two days ahead of schedule, he spotted the Trinity Shoals light buoy. That navigational marker allowed him to get an exact fix on his position — well outside American waters. On the morning of Wednesday, March 20, 1929, Randell dropped anchor. Chesley Hobbs reported some minor mechanical problems. Randell told him to make his repairs and be quick about it.

Hobbs had hardly begun work when Randell saw the *Walcott* coming toward them at top speed. "Heave up the anchor!" he ordered.

By the time the *I'm Alone* was under way, the *Walcott* was six miles off and closing at eleven knots. Because of the mechanical problems, the schooner could do only seven knots. Randell headed south. He saw the *Walcott* alter course, swinging into a big loop to intercept him.

The *Walcott* came up on the *I'm Alone*'s stern, blowing the signal to heave to. Randell ignored it. The *Walcott* moved up and hoisted signal flags that carried the command, "Heave to." Randell paid them no notice.

Then the *Walcott* came close enough for the commander, Warrant Officer Frank Paul, to hail by megaphone. "Heave to!"

Through his own megaphone, Randell replied, "I will not heave to. I'm on the high seas, and you have no jurisdiction over me."

Paul replied, "I'll have to open fire on you if you don't heave to."

Randell shouted back, "Shoot if you want to!"

The *Walcott* hung back, as though Paul wasn't sure what to do next. Then the cutter came close to the *I'm Alone* again. "Captain," Paul shouted through his megaphone, "I'd like to come aboard you for a talk."

Randell had a clear view of the *Walcott's* deck and didn't like what he saw. The gun crew had manned their four-pound cannon. One well-placed shot and the schooner would be finished. But Paul seemed reluctant to fire. Randell decided to talk to him.

"Captain, you may come aboard," he called, "but only with one man and unarmed."

Paul agreed. Randell ordered engines stopped. The *Walcott* came alongside the *I'm Alone*. But as the cutter's crew began to lower a boat, Randell saw the gunners load a shell into the cannon. One man had a hand on the lanyard. Several armed guardsmen were about to join Paul in the boat.

Randell ordered full speed ahead, and the schooner started to move. Randell called to Paul, "You can come aboard only if you follow my instructions to come with one man and both of you unarmed. Also, you've got to keep your gun crew away from that gun."

On Paul's orders the gun crew stood down and the escort fell back. Paul crossed to the schooner with just one man.

Randell welcomed Paul aboard with a handshake and invited him into his cabin. Paul asked why he had refused to heave to. Randell replied that he was in international waters. Then he added, "I knew that if I had allowed you to come on board with an armed guard, you would have seized the schooner and taken her in. Isn't that so?"

"Yes, Captain," Paul said, "those were my orders — to bring you in."

"Do you realize," Randell asked, "that the United States Coast Guard, officers and men, have been perjuring themselves lately by swearing that all vessels they have brought in were inside territorial waters, even if they were taken a hundred miles offshore?"

"I do not think that is true, Captain," Paul replied.

"Maybe you don't," Randell said, "but it is a well-known fact, and that is exactly what would happen to me if I allowed you to take me in. Why should I allow my owners to be put to the expense, the time, and trouble of trying to get the vessel clear again after she was seized?"

Then Randell asked, "Captain, just why do you wish to take in the *I'm Alone*?"

Paul replied, "Because you are inside the treaty limit."

Randell looked at Paul in astonishment and asked how he determined his position.

"I left the Trinity Shoals light buoy last night at nine o'clock," Paul said. "I have been waiting, drifting around, until I sighted you just after daybreak. I kept taking soundings. I knew my position within a quarter of a mile."

That wasn't what Randell expected to hear from a professional seaman. "I fail to see how you can possibly know it," he said, "with a two-knot current running, the sound-ings practically the same for thirty miles to the west, and you drifting all night by your own admission. Have you seen land? Have you determined your position by star-sights since you left the light buoy last night?"

Paul said he had no instruments for taking star-sights. Randell showed him his own sextant, which was equipped for star-sighting. Paul admitted he had never seen one like it.

Randell then showed Paul his chart, pointing out exactly where they were, and the course the *I'm Alone* had taken from the light buoy. Paul argued that Randell's calculations were off.

Randell produced a copy of the navigational treaty be-tween Great Britain and the United States that, he said, showed beyond a shadow of doubt that the *I'm Alone* was within the law. Paul said he didn't have a copy of that doc-ument on his ship. However, he did have a book of United States Coast Guard regulations that he claimed gave him the right to seize the *I'm Alone*.

The two captains examined each other's documents and disputed the fine points of clauses and regulations. Randell seemed to have finally won his argument, that the *I'm Alone* had not entered American waters, when Paul suddenly said, "Captain, you made a great mistake this morning. You threatened to shoot me if I came aboard you."

Randell denied making any such threat.

"If you did say it, it would go very hard with you if I took you in," Paul warned.

It seemed to Randell that Paul was now grasping at straws. "When you told me you would fire at me if I did not stop," he said, "the words I used were, 'Shoot if you want.' The only weapons I have on board are an old rifle and an old Colt six-shooter I carried in the Boer War that I keep as souvenirs."

Paul confessed that he didn't really believe Randell had any thought of shooting him. After almost two hours aboard the *I'm Alone,* he was ready to return to the *Walcott.* Thinking he had finally convinced Paul that he had broken no laws, he asked the Coast Guard officer to have a drink with him. "No, thanks," Paul said. "I never touch it."

Paul returned to the *Walcott.* He dropped back a short distance behind the schooner and radioed the Coast Guard base in Mobile, Alabama. Minutes later he ordered his crew to prepare to seize the *I'm Alone.* Paul had instructions to use whatever force was necessary.

At about two o'clock in the afternoon, the *Walcott* raced up to the *I'm Alone.* Once again, Randell saw the signal flags ordering him to heave to. He told a crewman to hoist the signal for "No." The *Walcott* came to within megaphone distance. Paul called out, "Captain, I have orders to take you in. I will give you fifteen minutes to make up your mind. If you do not stop, I will be obliged to fire at you."

Randell megaphoned back, "I have no intention of stopping. You need not waste the fifteen minutes."

Twenty minutes later, the *Walcott's* deck gun fired. No shell hit the *I'm Alone,* and Randell didn't see a splash. There was a second shot with the same result. Paul had fired blanks. But through his binoculars, Randell saw the gun crew reloading with what he knew was a live shell.

The cutter was only two hundred yards away. At that distance, the gunners couldn't miss. But when the big gun roared, the shell only pierced a sail. Paul was deliberately firing high.

The *Walcott* fired twenty rounds, putting more holes in the sails and cutting away rigging. Then the gun jammed. Paul barked some orders. A guardsman suddenly appeared on deck with a Thompson submachine gun. He took position behind the bulwarks and opened fire.

Men ducked for cover as bullets whizzed across the *I'm Alone*. Randell was almost knocked off his feet when he was hit in the right thigh. He staggered, and his whole leg went numb. He looked down expecting to see blood, but there wasn't any — not even a hole in his trousers. On the deck by his feet, he saw a hard wax bullet, the type police used to break up riots.

The *Walcott* ceased firing and dropped back a short distance. Randell continued on a southerly course. He was thankful that Paul hadn't sprayed the *I'm Alone* with real steel-jacketed bullets. But at sunset that day, Randell's sense of gratitude gave way to anger when, as was customary, he hauled down the *I'm Alone*'s flag. There was a hole in his Union Jack! No Newfoundlander, loyal to king and country, could tolerate such an insult. Randell wrote later, "If I had had a three-pounder aboard, that cutter would have gone to the bottom quick."

But Randell could only vent his outrage by signalling to Paul, "Captain, you have made a grave error. You have mutilated my flag."

For the next thirty-six hours, Randell sailed south by

east, heading for a point about twenty miles east of the Alacrán Reef off the coast of Mexico. The *Walcott* doggedly stayed on his tail. By daybreak of Friday, March 22, 1929, the winds had grown stronger and a heavy sea was running. At 7:30 a.m., at a point more than two hundred miles from the American coast, Randell sighted another cutter racing toward them. The *Dexter*.

The *Dexter* went alongside the *Walcott* and the commanders had a conference. Paul told Powell about his meeting with Randell. He said his deck gun was jammed, and he didn't think he had enough men to board the *I'm Alone* by force.

Paul said, "My advice is not to fire at the schooner. This weather is too rough. I'd wait until the wind moderates."

Powell replied, "To hell with them! I came to get them, and I'm going to get them."

At eight o'clock, the *Dexter* pulled away from the *Walcott* and roared up on Randell's starboard quarter. Powell flew signals that said, "Heave to or I fire at you."

Randell replied, "You have no jurisdiction over me and I refuse to stop."

"Hard-boiled" Powell didn't waste any time with warning shots, blanks, or wax bullets. A barrage of four-pounder explosive shells and a fusillade of rifle and machine gun bullets went shrieking across the water at the *I'm Alone* at a range of less than two hundred yards. They shredded the sails and rigging. Shells smashed through the schooner's upper works, destroying booms, bulwarks, and lifeboats.

The moment the *Dexter* opened fire, Randell hoisted his shell-torn Union Jack. A machine gunner on the *Dexter* tried to shoot it down. Nothing could have made Randell more defiant.

Randell and his men stood in a group on the aft deck. He noted later that the *Dexter's* riflemen and machine gunners did not shoot at the men, whom they could have picked off easily. None of the cannon shells had been aimed at the *I'm Alone's* waterline or below it.

After riddling the schooner, Powell ordered a ceasefire. He called to Randell, "Now will you stop?"

Enraged, Randell shouted back, "No, damn you! You may sink me if you like, but I will not surrender!"

Powell ordered his gunners to resume firing, and this time they aimed at the waterline. Shells smashed through the *I'm Alone's* hull. As water poured in, Randell asked his men if they were afraid. One man replied for them all. "Afraid! Hell no! Let the bastards sink her and be damned to them!"

"Skipper, don't stop 'em," Leon Maingoy said. "Let them sink her if they want, but don't you stop 'em."

John Williams agreed. "Skipper, we only die once! As long as we go down with that old flag flying, we've died for something."

Then Randell heard Powell shout at his chief gunner. The crew immediately slammed a series of shells straight into the *I'm Alone's* waterline, "as if they were sewing a seam," as Randell described it later.

The schooner slowed and began to settle bow first. All of the lifeboats had been smashed, so Randell ordered the men to throw overboard every bit of wreckage that could help them stay afloat. "Jump overboard!" he ordered. "Hang onto those broken dories. Just hang on and float."

Everyone jumped except Eddie Young. He clung to a rail in fear. Randell tore the man's grip loose, picked him up, and threw him over the side.

Standing alone on the aft deck, Randell waited until the bow was submerged and the stern rose ten feet in the air before he kicked off his shoes and jumped into the sea. When he came up, the *I'm Alone* was gone. Randell wrote later, "She went down with the British flag flying."

As he rose on the crest of a wave, Randell looked around. He saw his men swimming or clinging to pieces of wreckage. A cabin door, torn free as the *I'm Alone* plunged toward the bottom, broke the surface a few feet in front of him. Randell grabbed onto it and swam to the *Dexter.*

The *Dexter*'s crew hauled Randell and four more men aboard. A guardsman asked, "Have you got any arms or ammunition on you?"

Gasping, Randell said, "You must be crazy to think I'd try to swim in a sea like that with a revolver and ammunition!"

The man searched him anyway.

Nearby, the *Walcott* was fighting heavy swells as Paul tried to fish the rest of the *I'm Alone* crew out of the water. Two men were rescued, but a third slipped back into the sea. Seaman First Class Charles Raeburn dove in after him. In spite of the choppy seas, Raeburn managed to grab hold of the man and pull him onto a piece of debris.

The *Walcott* picked them both up. Randell had witnessed Raeburn's heroics, but he didn't know who the near-drowned man was.

Randell and his four crewmen were given dry clothing

and hot coffee, but he was concerned for the three on the *Walcott*. At his request, Powell sent a message asking if they were all right. The reply came that one man was unconscious and the crew was trying to revive him.

Later, Powell told Randell that the sailor Raeburn had pulled out of the sea was Leon Maingoy. He was conscious, Powell said, but very sick. Randell asked him to make all possible speed for port so Maingoy could be taken to a hospital. Powell ordered full speed ahead for New Orleans.

As the cutters headed north, a guardsman approached Randell with a set of leg shackles. "My orders are to put you in irons," he said.

"Am I a prisoner of war?" Randell asked.

"Never mind about that," the crewman replied. "It's orders."

"Whose orders?" asked Randell.

"Captain Powell's," the man replied as he clamped the irons around Randell's bare ankles.

Soon after, another guardsman stealthily handed Randell a pair of socks. "I noticed you were barefoot," he said. "Wad these between the irons and your ankles, Captain. Don't let the Old Man know I slipped them to you."

Twenty-four hours later the *Dexter* and the *Walcott* tied up at the United States Army Engineers wharf at the mouth of the Mississippi River. Randell wasn't permitted to go on deck. When Powell came below, Randell asked him how Maingoy was. Powell said he didn't know.

Paul came aboard to question Randell. "You tell me how that sick man of mine is getting along before I have a word to say to you about anything else," Randell demanded.

"He's getting along as well as can be expected," Paul replied.

Randell was exasperated. He said it was strange that they weren't making every effort to get Maingoy to hospital as quickly as possible. Paul left without another word.

A few hours later, the cutters were steaming upstream towards New Orleans. Although he was hobbled by his leg irons and under orders to stay below, Randell took the chance of going up on deck. He found a place by the rail that was out of sight of the bridge. A guardsman saw Randell, but instead of ordering him below or reporting him, gave him a cigarette.

Leaning on a rail while he smoked, Randell saw the signals that passed between the cutters. He could read them "as plain as print." A message from the *Walcott* said, "There's hell to pay ashore about this business. Tip your crowd to keep their mouths shut about the position of the *I'm Alone.*"

The *Dexter* replied, "Let them try to get it."

Clearly, the two Coast Guard commanders knew the sinking had been illegal.

At eight o'clock in the morning on Sunday, March 24, 1929, the cutters tied up at a New Orleans wharf. Randell's leg irons were removed, and he and his men were taken under armed guard to the United States Custom House. They entered through a back door to avoid a throng of reporters. Randell and the crewmen who'd been on the *Dexter* were kept apart from the ones who'd been on the *Walcott*. The prisoners weren't allowed to speak.

Inside, Randell met the Supervisor of Customs Mr. Creighton

and Captain A.L. Gamble, Base Commander of the United States Coast Guard for the Gulf of Mexico. Gamble began to question Randell, but Randell cut him off.

"Gentlemen, I wish to inform you that the sinking of my ship was a cowardly act, and that my crew and I were taken half-drowned out of the water more than two hundred miles from the coast of the United States of America. Under those circumstances, I claim that you have no jurisdiction over me or my men. We are ship-wrecked mariners. As such, I demand that I be allowed to get in touch with my consul and my owners, and immediately."

Creighton told Randell that he didn't think the British consul would want to have anything to do with him. Moreover, he said, there would be little likelihood of reaching him on a Sunday.

"My consul certainly knows of the sinking of the *I'm Alone*, since the newspaper reporters know about it," Randell said. "I am sure he will wish to see me and my men at the earliest opportunity."

Creighton promised to contact the British consul. Meanwhile, Randell and his men were held in the custom house where they were all questioned. The men from the *Walcott* were still kept apart from the others. Under pressure from customs officials, Randell reluctantly made a formal statement and signed it.

On Monday evening, Randell finally met Henry Tom, the British Consul General for the southern United States. Tom had been trying to get news of Randell and his crew since Saturday morning, when he first heard of the sinking.

After listening to Randell's account, he was surprised that the Americans had kept him in the dark for almost three days.

Then the Americans stunned Randell with the news that Leon Maingoy was dead when they pulled him out of the water. They said the *I'm Alone*'s survivors were being charged with conspiring to violate the Volstead Act and interfering with a customs officer in the performance of his duties. The men were taken to Orleans Parish Prison to await trial. Henry Tom engaged Edwin Grace, a New Orleans admiralty lawyer, as their counsel.

The sinking of the *I'm Alone* and Maingoy's death became international news. Reporters and photographers were allowed access to the prisoners, in spite of Creighton's efforts to keep them out. A photograph of Randell and his men behind bars that appeared in a London newspaper stirred up British anger. On March 26, Vincent Massey, Canada's senior envoy in Washington, requested that Henry L. Stinson, the American Secretary of State, provide the Canadian government with a statement of the facts concerning the *I'm Alone* incident. Massey received the statement two days later.

The official American position was that the *I'm Alone* had been half a mile inside American waters when first sighted by the *Walcott*. That meant the Coast Guard had the right to pursue the schooner into international waters. If the crew of the suspect vessel refused to stop, the Coast Guard commander had the legal right to open fire. It was later revealed that the Coast Guard wanted to make an example of the *I'm Alone* and subject Randell and his crew to a show trial. They would be convicted and sent to prison. That plan backfired.

On March 30, 1929, through the efforts of Tom and Grace, Randell was released on a five hundred dollar bond. His men were released without bail on their own recognizance. Money was wired to Randell, probably from Montreal. He took his men shopping for new clothes and then to a hotel for hot baths and a few drinks. Prohibition-era New Orleans was one of the "wettest" cities in the United States.

Meanwhile, the trouble over the *I'm Alone* incident heated up. There was no proof that the schooner had ever entered American waters. British and Canadian politicians called the attack an act of piracy. The *New York World* said the *Dexter* was unjustified in firing on the schooner. In New Orleans, *The Times-Picayune* called Randell a hero.

On April 10,, 1929, the charges against Randell and his crew were dismissed. Six years passed before the Canadian and American governments finally settled the dispute. Washington made a formal apology to Ottawa and paid the owners of the *I'm Alone* twenty-five thousand dollars. An additional twenty-five thousand dollars in compensation was paid to the captain and crew. Leon Maingoy's widow received ten thousand.

Captain Jack Randell spent the rest of his working life at sea. Poor health forced him to retire in 1941. He died at his home in Port Rexton in 1944. Randell's encounter with the United States Coast Guard made him and the *I'm Alone* legendary in Newfoundland. Canadian song-writer Wade Hemsworth immortalized man and ship in his ballad, "The Story of the *I'm Alone.*" In the published lyrics, Randell's name is spelled *Randall*.

Oh, I'm Alone,
A long way from Lunenburg she went down
Because Skipper John Randall wouldn't heave to
On the I'm Alone

Lyrics from "The Story of the *I'm Alone*" are from
The Songs of Wade Hemsworth, edited by Hugh Verrier,
Penumbra Press, 1990, with permission.

6

Saint-Pierre: The Chicago Connection

The Prohibition years were a golden age for Saint Pierre and Miquelon, about fifteen miles off the south coast of Newfoundland. Officially part of France, the islands were beyond the jurisdiction of Canadian and American liquor laws. They were a safe haven for rum-runners operating between the Atlantic Provinces and the eastern seaboard of the United States.

Fishing was the islands' main legal economic activity, but after the Great War, independent fishermen couldn't compete with the big steam trawlers. Saint Pierrais turned to their other main economic activity — *la fraude*. Smuggling had been going on for generations, and it boomed in the 1920s.

In the port town of Saint-Pierre, warehouses that had been sitting empty were suddenly packed with cases of liquor from Canada, Britain, and France. Fishermen who had eked out a meagre living from the sea abandoned their boats to earn hard cash as stevedores, unloading and loading cargoes of booze at the docks. In a single month, three hundred thousand cases of alcoholic beverages passed through Saint-Pierre. The business transactions that took place on the island were all perfectly legal, providing the local government with a windfall of millions of dollars in taxes. The funds were used for public works such as road construction and two fresh water reservoirs.

A big fish-processing plant called La Frigorifique was converted into a warehouse to handle the overflow of merchandise. Even the old French Navy disciplinary barracks became storage space for liquor. Some islanders even constructed houses from the wood from cast-off liquor cases.

As Saint-Pierre's importance as a centre in the rum-running business grew, residents found themselves hosting a succession of unusual visitors. Gangsters from big American cities arrived to purchase liquor by the shipload and arrange transportation to the United States. The "businessmen" with their American accents stood out in their natty three-piece suits that concealed pistols tucked into shoulder holsters. They were friendly, and free with the money they peeled from large wads of bills. They bought meals for poor warehouse workers, and one even donated five thousand dollars to the town's priest for the construction of a new school.

The hoodlums posed no problems for the local police, a few gendarmes from France, and the police didn't harass them. The constables were more likely to keep an eye out for secret agents of the American government who used clandestine radio transmissions to tip off US customs vessels about the departure of rum-runners. The gangsters were regarded as Robin Hoods and treated like foreign dignitaries.

One American mobster who took a special interest in Saint-Pierre was Chicago's Dean O'Banion. He was the leader of the notorious North Side Gang. O'Banion was a powerful crime boss with considerable political influence in Chicago. He had customers for his illegal alcohol in some of Chicago's wealthiest neighbourhoods. He peddled Canadian whiskey to working-class Chicagoans, but his more well-heeled clients wanted beverages that could be served in crystal glasses on silver trays in the mansions of Chicago's elite. O'Banion needed a reliable source for the best French wines and brandies, and he wanted to cut out the American middlemen who had been supplying him. In the summer of 1924, he sent one of his chief lieutenants to Saint-Pierre. The French islanders would be surprised to learn that this American gangster could converse with them in their own language.

George Moran was a major underworld figure in Prohibition Chicago. He got the nickname "Bugs," which he hated, because of his hair-trigger temper. Although Italian gangsters like Al Capone referred to him as "that Mick bastard," Moran wasn't Irish.

Moran's real name was Adelard Leo Cunin. He was born in St. Paul, Minnesota, in 1891. His father, Jules, was a blacksmith who had emigrated from France. His mother, Marie Diana, was from St. Alphonse, Quebec. French was the language spoken in the Cunin household.

Adelard grew up in a working-class neighbourhood of

St. Paul that had a large French-Canadian population, derisively called Frogtown by Anglophone outsiders. He was a tough kid with a deep dislike of discipline and authority. He fell in with juvenile gangs, getting an early start on the road to being a career criminal. At the age of eighteen, Adelard was sent to Minnesota's state juvenile correction facility on a robbery conviction. He escaped less than a year later.

Adelard fled to Chicago where he joined a burglary gang. During a robbery in 1910, he was shot in the back by a night watchman, captured, and sentenced to a term in Joliet Prison. To conceal the fact that he was wanted as an escapee in Minnesota, he gave his name as George Miller. From that point, "Adelard Cunin" vanished from official records.

Adelard was released on parole in 1912. Before the year was out, he was arrested in Chicago on charges of grand larceny and receiving stolen goods. This time, he told the police and the courts that his name was George Moran. He was sent back to Joliet Prison where he remained until 1917. After his release, Adelard used other aliases, but George "Bugs" Moran was the name that stuck.

Moran kept his family background a secret, partly to throw Minnesota authorities off his trail, but also to protect the honour and name of his parents, who had since moved to Manitoba. Not many of Moran's criminal associates were aware that he spoke fluent French.

Moran met O'Banion in 1917. These two, along with hoodlums Vincent "The Schemer" Drucci and Earl Wojciechowski (alias Hymie Weiss), made up the core of the notorious North Side Gang. The Northsiders were involved in robbery, gambling, extortion, and just about every other racket with the exception of prostitution, which devout Catholic O'Banion considered immoral. When Prohibition became law in 1920, O'Banion's mob was quick to start milking the cash cow the American government had blindly handed to well-organized criminals.

As rival Chicago gangs fought over bootlegging turf, two emerged as the strongest: O'Banion's Northsiders, and the Southsiders led by Johnny Torrio and his fearsome chief enforcer, Al Capone. But while hired thugs and gunmen clashed in the streets, the gang leaders went about the complex business of the international bootleg trade. While buying off police chiefs, judges, and politicians, they had to make contacts with suppliers in Canada, the Caribbean, Britain, and continental Europe. They had to arrange for transportation of their product into the United States. The fundamental necessities of smuggling took the agents of big operators like O'Banion and Torrio to small port towns on the Great Lakes, lonely crossing points on the border between Canada and the United States, and exotic, out-of-the-way locations such as Saint-Pierre.

By 1924, Moran was one of O'Banion's closest confidants. O'Banion would have certainly known that he was bilingual. Sending Moran to Saint-Pierre would have been a practical measure for O'Banion. He wouldn't naively trust the liquor merchants on the island. Moran's knowledge of French ensured that he would understand every word spoken in his presence.

There is no documented record of Moran's business

activities in Saint-Pierre. For obvious reasons, men like him didn't leave paper trails. However, Rose Keefe, a Nova Scotia–born author and Moran's biographer, interviewed a former Saint-Pierraise who, as a young girl, had met him.

"One day we saw two men standing around near the old plant. I could tell immediately that they were visitors, probably American, because they were so well dressed. They had their hands in their pockets and acted like they were waiting for someone. One of them, the taller one, saw us and approached. I was immediately nervous because I didn't speak any English and I was afraid he would ask me something.

"Imagine my shock when he spoke to me in very good French. He had a strange accent and he used some expressions that I'd never heard, but I had no difficulty understanding him. He told me that he and his friend were here to keep an appointment, but the man they wanted to see was late. He asked me if my friends and I could run and get them a couple of bottles of ale, I think it was. If we would, we could keep the change from the big bill he gave us . . . I don't think he told us his name, as we were only kids, but he did say he was from America. I guessed him to be Quebecois from his accent."

Not until years later did the girl learn that the American with the Quebecois accent was Bugs Moran. She saw his photograph in a newspaper story about one of the most spectacular crimes in American history — the St. Valentine's Day Massacre.

Friction between the North Side and South Side Gangs in Chicago had been heating up even before Moran went to Saint-Pierre. It exploded into all-out gang warfare in November 1924, when South Side gunmen murdered O'Banion. In the following months, the two gangs turned Chicago into a war zone. After being badly shot up in a North Side ambush, Torrio fled Chicago, leaving Capone as the South Side boss. His gunmen killed Weiss. Then police shot Drucci dead. That left Bugs Moran as the boss of the North Side Gang and the number one target on Capone's hit list.

Moran recruited some of the deadliest hoodlums in Chicago to continue the fight against Capone. The gang war raged and the body count mounted, earning Chicago the title of murder capital of the United States.

Meanwhile, the embattled gangs raked in enormous profits from their bootlegging operations. The Northsiders benefited from Moran's contacts in Saint-Pierre. If the socialites of Chicago's exclusive Gold Coast district wanted genuine French champagne and cognac, they had to buy it from Moran. The public generally turned a deaf ear and a blind eye to the violence in Chicago. But the headline-making event of February 14, 1929, would bring about a dramatic change that affected not only Chicago and the United States, but also distant Saint-Pierre.

On that St. Valentine's Day morning, four men entered a North Side Gang garage. Two of them wore police uniforms. Inside were seven of Moran's men. One bore a resemblance to Moran and wore a hat and overcoat similar to the ones Bugs was known to wear.

The intruders were Capone hitmen. Posing as police, they lined the Northsiders up against a wall and then mowed them down with machine guns. The killers made their getaway in a vehicle disguised as a police car, thinking they had killed Bugs Moran. But Moran had stopped for a cup of coffee on his way to the garage and had missed a bloody death by minutes.

The St. Valentine's Day Massacre was, at the time, the biggest mass murder in modern American history. Nobody doubted that Al Capone was behind it, but he had an alibi. He was in Florida on February 14.

Moran's power as a big-time gangster declined in the wake of the massacre. He still operated as a bootlegger, but on a smaller scale and outside Chicago. Capone was now the gangster king of Chicago, but his days were numbered.

The mass slaying shocked the nation. Many Americans had always thought Prohibition to be a mistake. Now the bloody massacre increased public pressure for its repeal. That finally happened in 1933. By that time, Capone was in prison, brought down on charges of tax evasion.

The demise of Prohibition was a serious blow to Saint-Pierre's economy, but it didn't immediately end the town's role in liquor smuggling. Shiploads of alcohol still left Saint-Pierre, bound for the coasts of Canada and the United States, where the cargoes were smuggled ashore past customs agents and sold by black-market bootleggers. The government of France shut that practice down in 1935 when, under pressure from Ottawa and Washington, it decreed that all alcoholic exports from Saint-Pierre must be bonded.

Moran engaged in various illegal activities after the repeal of Prohibition, but he was never again the big shot he'd been when he visited Saint-Pierre. Moran ended his criminal career as a bank robber. He was captured and convicted. He died from cancer in Leavenworth Federal Penitentiary on February 25, 1957.

Adelard Cunin, alias George "Bugs" Moran, son of a French father and a French Canadian mother, was buried in a prison cemetery. But he would have a place in American legend as the gangster Al Capone failed to kill. In the lore of Saint-Pierre, he is one of those shadowy American strangers who came in the glory days of *la fraude*.

7

The *Josephine K* Affair: Death of a Rum-Runner

On Christmas Eve, 1930, Captain William P. "Billy" Cluett told his friend Reverend W.E. Ryder that he was "dissatisfied with the game, and ready to get out of it." They were in St. John's Church in Lunenburg, Nova Scotia, where Cluett was attending a watchnight service with his wife June. Ryder had married them in that church six years earlier, and now they had two sons, ages three and five. June was expecting their third child. The "game" Cluett wanted out of was rum-running.

Cluett was born in Belleoram, Newfoundland. He was twenty-two years old when he married June and decided to make Lunenburg his home. He rose through the ranks in the coastal trade and earned a solid reputation as a seaman, and then as a skipper. Every crewman who sailed with Captain Cluett liked him.

Cluett faithfully attended Sunday services when he was ashore. He even wrote a special prayer that his wife and children could recite with him. But Cluett's piety didn't prevent him from taking advantage of the opportunity American Prohibition offered.

Lunenburg was a major Nova Scotia base for rum-running. Cluett would have learned from other Lunenburg skippers about the fast money to be made smuggling liquor into the United States and the risks involved, and the methods for evading the U.S. Coast Guard cutters.

In 1927 or 1928, Cluett became captain of the *Josephine K*, a propeller-driven vessel that had formerly been in auxiliary service in the Royal Navy. The *Josephine K* was large enough to carry several thousand cases of liquor. In good weather, she could make a respectable fourteen knots. The *Josephine K* was registered in Digby, Nova Scotia, to the Liverpool Shipping Company. However, it's possible that Cluett was working for the same businessmen who had employed Jack Randell.

The *Josephine K* would pick up cargoes of liquor in Saint-Pierre, and then make runs to Boston, New York City, and Atlantic City. Sometimes Cluett stayed outside American territorial waters and delivered contraband to motorboats. Once, he sneaked right into the Atlantic City harbour at night, and collided with a drawbridge. With a hole punched in his bow, he still managed to escape to the open sea.

On another smuggling run, the *Josephine K* ran onto a Sable Island sandbar. She was stuck fast, weighed down by a full cargo of liquor. Heavy seas broke over her, tearing away the lifeboats and the pilot house. One crewman said later, "I didn't look to see the land anymore."

Cluett managed to free his vessel from the trap and made his delivery. But he must have wondered if he was pushing his luck. By that time he had been in the smuggling business for three years. The Coast Guard had never caught him, even though they had marked the *Josephine K* as a smuggler. Like every other captain in eastern Canada, Cluett would have read the newspaper stories about the sinking of the *I'm Alone.*

Cluett told Reverend Ryder that he was getting out while the getting was good. He was "fairly comfortable" financially, and planned on quitting at the end of January. Right after Christmas, Cluett was off to Saint-Pierre to begin a month of ferrying booze down to America's Rum Coast.

In late January 1931, the *Josephine K* picked up a cargo of liquor at Saint-Pierre. Cluett's crew of eight men included his mate, a Newfoundlander named Wesley Anderson; a sailor named Allen Falkenham; and Cluett's younger brother Alfred, who was on his first smuggling voyage. The captain had said that this would be his final trip.

In the early evening of January 24, 1931 near the Ambrose Channel off New York City, the *Josephine K* was unloading cargo onto the barge *Brooklyn* and the tugboat *Dauntless*, which had towed the barge out from Newark, New Jersey. While the unloading was in progress, a speedboat full of men from New York City arrived on the scene. Minutes later, Cluett and his crew heard the unmistakable sound of the engine of an approaching Coast Guard cutter. Cluett ordered his men to cut the cables lashing the *Josephine K* to the *Brooklyn* and made a run for it. What happened next depends on whose testimony one chooses to believe.

Chief Boatswain Karl Schmidt, a veteran officer, was the commander of Coast Guard patrol boat No. 145 (CG-145). He said in his report that he had been patrolling in the vicinity of the Lightship *Ambrose* when his first mate, Wilbur Tally, spotted a speedboat heading out from New York. Suspecting that the boat was going to rendezvous with a rum-runner, Schmidt followed it. Darkness was falling, and the men in the boat were apparently unaware that the patrol boat was behind them.

When CG-145 approached the suspect vessels, the men from the speedboat were already aboard the *Brooklyn.* Schmidt saw a ship pull away and head east. They were unarguably inside American waters, so Schmidt decided to pursue the vessel and stop her before she reached the open sea. He sent radio messages to other Coast Guard cutters in the area to come to his assistance.

CG-145 pulled alongside the fleeing rum-runner and sounded the klaxon horn. When there was no response, Schmidt fired three blanks from his one-pounder deck gun. That warning was also ignored. The cutter's gunners then put three shots across the fugitive's bow — an ultimatum to heave to immediately, or else!

The vessel didn't stop, so Schmidt ordered his gun crew to disable her with two shots amidships. The cutter's gun roared twice. The shells hit their target and the ship slowed to a stop. Schmidt reported that it was only when he came close enough to sweep the vessel with his searchlight, that he saw the name *Josephine K* and realized he had caught a notorious rum-runner. At that time, he heard an angry voice from the stricken vessel cry, "You lousy bastard! You shot a man!"

Schmidt boarded the *Josephine K* with an armed party. He found Captain Cluett lying on deck in a pool of blood. Part of one leg had been blown away. Schmidt immediately took action to save Cluett's life. He put Tally in charge of the armed squad on the *Josephine K*, with orders to hold her at anchor or drift until he returned. Then he had Cluett transferred to CG-145. Schmidt radioed his base, requesting that a boat with a doctor be sent out to meet the cutter.

Near the Lightship *Ambrose*, CG-145 met CG-180, commanded by Chief Boatswain's Mate James Axel. Schmidt wanted to put Cluett on CG-180 to be taken to the New York Coast Guard base, but the swell was too heavy and his condition too serious for him to be transferred. Instead, Schmidt and Axel temporarily exchanged commands. Axel would take CG-145 to the base, keeping an eye out for the boat with the doctor. Schmidt would take CG-180 to go back after the suspect vessels. Then a third cutter, CG-161, arrived. Schmidt hailed the commander, Boatswain Herbert Matthews, and told him to go to the *Josephine K* and stay with her while he rounded up the others.

As Schmidt had expected, the other vessels had fled the unloading location while he was chasing the *Josephine K*. The men in the speedboat had made their getaway, but the tugboat and barge hadn't gone very far. Schmidt boarded the *Brooklyn* with an armed party and found sacks of liquor on deck and in the hold. The barge's skipper, Mario Landi, told him a colourful tale.

Landi claimed that he had been returning from dumping a load of garbage when a speedboat full of armed men pulled up alongside. They commandeered his barge at gunpoint and forced him and his two crewmen into the pump room. Then the *Josephine K* came alongside and started unloading contraband. There was so much of it, Landi said, that he was afraid the barge would capsize. He protested, but the gunmen told him to shut up. Then they started loading sacks into the speedboat. The sudden arrival of the Coast Guard interrupted the hijacking, and the *Josephine K* fled.

After listening to Landi's story, Schmidt had him and his men put under arrest, along with the skipper and crew of the tugboat. He seized the *Brooklyn* and the *Dauntless* and took three sacks of liquor as evidence. He left some guardsmen in charge and then proceeded at full speed to the *Josephine K*.

Schmidt found the rum-runner riding at anchor under the surveillance of CG-161. He went aboard and found that Tally had the crew confined in the forecastle. There was still contraband liquor in the hold, but a search turned up no ship's manifest. The *Josephine K* had to be towed to New York because one of CG-145's shots had damaged her steering gear and the crew had deliberately disabled the engine.

The crews of the *Josephine K*, the *Brooklyn*, and the *Dauntless* were all jailed. They were soon released on bail posted by the Liverpool Shipping Company through their New York lawyer, Louis Halle. The bail for Wesley Anderson, nominally in command of the *Josephine K* in Captain

Cluett's absence, was highest at $7,500. The value of the confiscated liquor was estimated at $300,000.

Meanwhile, a fast Coast Guard motor launch with a doctor aboard did meet CG-145, so Cluett received medical treatment before the cutter reached New York. The vessel docked at the Coast Guard's Staten Island base, and an ambulance rushed him to Marine Hospital. Unfortunately, Cluett had lost too much blood and died at about two o'clock in the morning on January 25, 1931.

The story that Anderson gave to the New York press contradicted Schmidt's account. Anderson claimed that the *Josephine K* and the other vessels had been outside American territorial waters when CG-145 showed up. He said there had been no warning shots. During the entire incident, the cutter's deck gun had fired just three shots, all of them directly at the *Josephine K*. The first shell struck the vessel amidships. The second destroyed the lifeboat.

Anderson said he ducked into the engine room, and heard the third shot. When he came out, he saw that it had torn through the pilot house, where Captain Cluett was. He found Cluett on the deck, where he had dragged himself from the wreckage of the pilot house. A large piece of one thigh had been ripped away, but he was still conscious. Anderson was trying to administer first aid when Schmidt and his boarding party stepped onto the ship.

Anderson claimed that Schmidt was drunk. He said he heard Schmidt tell one of his men, "Don't let those fellows give me any more liquor. I'm too drunk now."

Then, according to Anderson, Schmidt stuck a pistol in Allen Falkenham's ribs and threatened to shoot him.

Another guardsman told Schmidt, "You'd better leave him alone. You're in trouble enough already."

Anderson's story was corroborated by all of the *Josephine K*'s crew. Years later, in an interview with Nova Scotia historian Ted R. Hennigar, Falkenham stated that Schmidt ignored the crewmen's pleas to get Cluett to a hospital as quickly as possible. He said an hour passed before Cluett was transferred to the cutter. Falkenham also said that the men in the speedboat weren't hijackers, but hired help who had been sent to speed up the transfer of cargo from the *Josephine K* to the *Brooklyn*.

Coming so soon in the wake of the *I'm Alone* controversy, the *Josephine K* case became another international incident. The government of Prime Minister R.B. Bennett wanted assurances that the Coast Guard had acted within the law. The Coast Guard, which had been fighting a losing battle against the rum-runners, had to justify Schmidt's actions.

Two days after Cluett's death, an official inquest was held in New York. Karl Schmidt denied that he'd been drinking and his crewmen supported his statement. One guardsman, Bennett Walker, said that one of the *Josephine K*'s crewmen told him, "If Captain Cluett dies, your skipper will die, too."

Schmidt said he did everything possible to get Cluett to the hospital quickly. He said he had no doubt that the rum-runner vessels were well within the American territorial limit when he came upon them. He had noted the position based on soundings and the distance from the Lightship *Ambrose*. However, his record of the location differed from that of one of the other cutter commanders.

The question then arose as to whether it had been necessary for Schmidt to use deadly force to stop Cluett's ship. The *Josephine K* and CG-145 were taken out for speed trials. The tests showed that the cutter was the faster vessel and could have overtaken the *Josephine K*. But Schmidt repeated his claim that he had fired six warning shots. Cluett's failure to heave to had left him with no alternative but to fire at the ship.

The inquest concluded that the officers and men of the Coast Guard had carried out their duties entirely within the law. Assistant Secretary of the Treasury Seymour Lowman said, "It is regrettable that the captain lost his life, but that was simply an incident to the transaction." The Canadian government lodged no official complaint and didn't demand any further investigation.

The Americans dropped the charges against the crew of the *Josephine K*, and they were allowed to return home. The ship remained impounded in New York pending legal proceedings. Alfred Cluett accompanied the casket containing his brother's body back to Nova Scotia.

Captain Cluett's funeral, held on February 1, 1931, was one of the biggest Lunenburg had ever seen. It was covered by reporters from Canada's major newspapers. Among the mourners who filled St. John's Church was Angus Walters, captain of the legendary schooner, the *Bluenose*. Reverend Ryder delivered a eulogy in which he praised Cluett as a seaman, friend, husband, and father. Six weeks later, June Cluett gave birth to a boy.

The *Josephine K* was forfeited to the United States

government. In the book *Rum War at Sea*, the United States Coast Guard's official authorized account of the Prohibition Era, Karl Schmidt's story of what happened when he encountered the *Josephine K* is the accepted version. The book does not say that Captain Cluett died, only that he was injured. However, in Reverend Ryder's sermon, which was printed in papers across Canada, Cluett's death was "nothing more nor less than murder on the high seas" and "one of the inevitable tragedies that follow the hypocrisy of prohibition."

PART III
CROOKS AND KILLERS

8

The Kellums of Halifax: Jail for the Winter

Comedian Red Skelton created a classic silent sketch in which his character, Freddie the Freeloader, tries to get himself arrested on Christmas Eve so he can spend Christmas in a warm jail cell where he'll be fed. It's a brilliant depiction of human pathos because, although Freddie is a shiftless tramp, he isn't a criminal. He bungles his attempts to break the law.

Skelton's hilarious creation was based on a social reality. In the Victorian and Edwardian periods in communities across Canada, people living on the margins saw the local jail as a refuge against the winter cold. Some were petty criminals. Others, in an age before social safety nets, were mentally ill or were, for a variety of reasons, victims of chronic poverty. Jail for the winter became an annual routine in their strategy for survival. Perhaps nobody was more adept at it than the Kellums of Halifax.

As the largest city in Atlantic Canada, Halifax had all

the urban problems of the Victorian age: slums, poverty, unemployment, and subsequently, crime. Halifax was a tough town for the underprivileged. The poorer quarters had high rates of illiteracy, domestic violence, and alcoholism. Many residents lived in substandard dwellings that lacked plumbing. Their homes stank in the summer and froze in the winter. Charitable agencies as they existed at the time were strained. Moreover, the general condescending attitude toward the poor was further tainted by racial prejudice — and the Kellums were black.

The patriarch of the family was Charles Kellum (also spelled Killum and Killam), whose name appears briefly in mid-nineteenth-century Halifax criminal records. He is believed to have been the father of John, Charles, Henry, Martha, and Mary Kellum. John, born about 1840, was the eldest. He was the family member for whom the most detailed documentation survives, thanks to his having been incarcerated more than a hundred times between 1857 and 1903.

John Kellum was first sent to jail on an assault conviction. Over the years, he and his brothers would find themselves behind bars for many of the "underclass" offences that filled police registers and court records: petty larceny, common assault, gambling, vagrancy, public drunkenness, disorderly conduct, assaulting police, and soliciting charity under false pretences. Living in a city with a busy harbour and a garrison, impoverished women like the Kellum sisters occasionally wound up in jail on prostitution charges. Even after the establishment of industrial schools for juvenile offenders, young Kellums were sent to jail because the new institutions were not for "people of colour."

The jail the Kellums came to know so well was Rock-head Prison, built in the North End of Halifax in 1854. It was an imposing structure of stone walls and barred windows that ironically had a spectacular view of Bedford Basin. Inmates were kept in cramped cells where the only furnishing was a cot. They worked on the prison farm or in a nearby quarry breaking rocks for construction projects. Sometimes they were put to work repairing roads in town.

When John Kellum was in his twenties and thirties, he didn't like going to jail any more than the next man. After all, it meant a period of hard labour. But heavy drinking and habitual thievery kept landing him in Rockhead. Family strife also kept the prison doors swinging open and closed because the Kellums frequently charged each other with assault and robbery. John was once given such a bad beating by his siblings that he showed signs of being mentally unbalanced.

John Kellum's jail sentences usually ranged from twenty to ninety days, although on one occasion a magistrate sent him to Rockhead for a year. There was one incident for which he pleaded not guilty to a charge of stealing several bottles of liquor, and friends provided him with an alibi. However, a man who allegedly had been Kellum's partner in the theft fell ill, and police claimed that on his deathbed he confessed to the crime and also named Kellum. John was hauled off to jail professing his innocence and threatening to sue. He would accept punishment when he knew he deserved it, but considered wrongful imprisonment an insult to his honour.

Kellum was sometimes employed as a whitewasher, coating fences and walls with a thin, paint-like solution made from slaked lime and chalk. Whitewashing, done with a broad brush or broom, was considered menial labour, suitable only for the lowest of the working class. Sometimes not even that was available to people in Halifax's black community, and they had to stoop to employment that was even more degrading.

When the Washburn Circus visited Halifax in 1897, John Kellum took a job in a sideshow game. Fair-goers got a chance to win a prize by throwing balls at John's head at five cents for three shots. The balls must have been hard, perhaps made of India rubber, because one of them caused a serious injury to his collarbone. Kellum spent his meagre pay on alcohol to dull the pain and the humiliation.

Because women weren't hired as whitewashers, the Kellum sisters, whose brothers and male partners usually couldn't be relied upon for support, had to find other sources of income. The court record for one of Martha's arrests gives her occupation as "berry picker." In season, Halifax's poor could earn a few cents a day in the blueberry fields. More often, the Kellum women pilfered food and merchandise from stores and engaged in the sex trade. Both sisters were arrested for being inmates of bawdy houses. Martha spent three-and-a-half years in Dorchester Penitentiary for viciously attacking another woman and biting off a piece of her ear.

It wasn't until John Kellum was approaching middle age that he began to look upon Rockhead as a regular winter refuge. He had periodically spent time in the county poor-house, but the strict regime wasn't to his liking. Kellum sometimes found himself homeless in the winter because he'd been evicted from his residence. On one occasion, he was on the street because his family kicked him out. Other times, he sought shelter at Rockhead because even jail was better than the cold, miserable hovel in which he'd been living.

To get there, Kellum would commit petty crimes for the singular purpose of being sent to jail. An associate in this scheme was a relative named George Deminas. George once stole a quilt off a clothesline just to earn himself a few months in Rockhead.

Kellum and Deminas were such regular winter guests in the prison that one November they decided to dispense with the obligatory crime and use basic logic. They went to the Halifax police station and asked to be "sent home." They said there was no whitewashing or any other work they could do to earn money. Sooner or later, they explained, they'd be accused of stealing, and then there would be a big fuss in the newspaper about it. The police would be doing them a favour, and saving themselves a lot of trouble, if they would arrange a six-month sentence for two. The request was granted.

Although the Kellums quarrelled, sometimes violently, they were fundamentally a close-knit family, just as ready to come to one another's assistance as they were to brawl. On some occasions when one had been arrested and jail time wasn't convenient, a brother or sister would go to court to provide an alibi. Once, when Martha was sentenced to a term in Rockhead, Mary asked to be sent with her because she said she couldn't bear to be parted from her sister. Henry was once told that John had died in prison and was inconsolable until he learned the news was untrue. John's siblings soon followed his example in making Rockhead their winter home.

In return for accommodation, the Kellums and Deminas kept the police informed of some of the activities of the Halifax underworld. They quietly passed along tips about bootleggers and establishments that violated liquor laws. John was even instrumental in preventing a man from hanging himself in a barn north of Maynard Street.

Undercover police work and suicide intervention notwithstanding, the Kellums' main civic contribution was whitewashing. They had an unofficial pact with the jail authorities whereby they would whitewash public buildings in return for winter room and board. John was often in charge of the whitewashing teams. The prison governor said he was a good worker and "an artist with the whitewash brush." Henry Kellum once referred to his clan as the "whitewashin' club."

However, sometimes the Kellums' plans didn't work out the way they had intended. In 1880, William Murray took charge as Rockhead's new governor. He decided it was in the best interest of justice and the community to make the prison uncomfortable for the regular residents. Murray's harsh regime of hard labour and scanty meals didn't appeal to Henry Kellum. He escaped rather than stay in a jail where, he complained, times weren't as good as they used to be and people starved. Henry was disappointed another time when he was sent to Rockhead in September. He was expecting a long stay but was released before he could enjoy a Christmas dinner in jail. Over time, however, Governor Murray grew to know the Kellums well and said that John was one of the most trustworthy men who had ever been in the prison.

In spite of such unfortunate setbacks as the ones Henry experienced, the Kellums were successful in making jail a sanctuary in what was, for them, a hostile environment. There is even documentation of an episode of preplanning. During one winter, Rockhead was infested with rats. The vermin scurried along the corridors and invaded the cells. The following October, in anticipation of their forthcoming winter residence, John Kellum and George Deminas rounded up ten stray cats and turned them loose in the prison yard.

To the city magistrates, the Kellums were a common nuisance. One judge became exasperated when Martha, who'd been brought before him on a minor charge, began haggling with him over the length of her jail sentence. He finally asked her how many days she felt she deserved. She said, "Well, say twenty, please." The judge immediately responded, "All right. Forty days! Who's next?"

However, the press began to regard John as a colourful character. The Halifax *Morning Chronicle* said he was a harmless fellow who sometimes assisted the police. The main cause of his troubles, the papers claimed, was his notorious family.

When several Kellums were incarcerated together, they would give concerts at which they sang, danced, and joked.

Their musical repertoire included old favourites such as "Sweet Bye and Bye", "I've Been Redeemed", and "Don't Be Weary, Children". They would also give renditions of local ballads, perhaps of their own composition, such as "It's Up To Rockhead We're Bound To Go." The papers would report that the Kellums "made the air sweet with melody and gay with dancing."

While the prison authorities and the press developed a patronizing attitude toward the Kellums, John in particular, the unfortunate fact remained that their situation in the community was so precarious that jail was a haven for them. Of course, Halifax wasn't the only Canadian city in which ethnic minorities occupied the lowest rung on the social ladder with little opportunity of climbing to a more acceptable level. Similar situations existed with First Nations and European and Asian immigrant communities across the country.

In the last years of his life, John Kellum's health deteriorated and he was unable to work. He became a permanent resident of the county poorhouse, where he is believed to have died on February 26, 1905. However, official records of the time are imprecise, and he might have drowned in Halifax Harbour in March of that year. Red Skelton's Freddie the Freeloader routine half a century later was a classic example of the definition of comedy as tragedy plus time.

9

Thomas Collins: The Stranger Did It

Nobody in the little community of New Ireland in Albert County, New Brunswick, knew anything about Thomas Francis Collins. He arrived in mid-August 1906, claiming to be a twenty-one-year-old sailor from a poor Irish neighbourhood in Liverpool, England. He said he'd only recently arrived in Canada.

Collins stood just five foot four, but his small frame was solid. He had a boyish face, a winning smile, and a friendly personality. That might have been why the parish priest, Father Edward J. MacAulay, took pity on him, a lad who was alone and penniless in a strange country. MacAulay offered Collins a job at the rectory for which he would receive room and board and seven dollars a month. Collins cheerfully accepted.

As pastor of the rural parish of St. Agatha, MacAulay didn't have much money to spare for hired help. His live-in housekeeper, Mary Ann MacAulay, was a second cousin who had never married. She had been with him for twenty-five years. Father MacAulay paid her one hundred and twenty dollars a year plus room and board for which she did the cooking, laundry, and other chores. It had been a practical and satisfactory arrangement for them both. Mary Ann was frugal and kept a sharp eye on the rectory's finances. She also spent little money on herself. Her one indulgence was a lady's gold watch.

But Mary Ann was now fifty-two years old. Father MacAulay was sixty-two, and feeling his age more every day. He thought it was about time he hired someone to help with the chores. A cheerful lad like Collins would be good company for Mary Ann during times when the priest did the rounds of his extensive parish and was away for days. She didn't like being in the rectory alone and would stay with neighbours. In addition, three weeks earlier, while they were both out of the house, a burglar had broken in and stolen some bottles of whiskey and sacramental wine.

But it soon became obvious that Collins was unfamiliar with the kind of work required of him. He didn't know anything about horses and had never handled any of the kind of tools in the rectory woodshed. Nonetheless, Father MacAulay had faith in him and told a parishioner, "He doesn't seem to know how to do anything, but after he learns, he'll be quite a smart boy."

Mary Ann didn't share MacAulay's optimism. She didn't think they could afford a hired man in the first place, let alone one who didn't even know how to hitch up a horse. Mary Ann had been running the house for years, and now there was a stranger living in it.

Mary Ann treated Collins civilly in Father MacAulay's presence, but in the priest's absence she browbeat him and called him a fool. She refused to serve him meals until he had performed tasks precisely to her satisfaction. If he didn't do a job right, she scolded him. On one occasion, Mary Ann sent Collins fishing with some local men so he could bring back some trout for her to prepare for supper. When he returned with a much smaller catch than the others, she chastised him. Collins never complained to Father MacAulay, but he began to regret accepting the job at the rectory.

A fortnight after he had hired Collins, Father MacAulay left for a five-day tour of his parish. Travelling by train, mail wagon, and buggy, he did the rounds of farms and villages. On August 20, 1906, he was on the homeward leg of his trip when he stopped in the little community of Elgin, about eight miles from New Ireland. He was surprised to run into Collins at Garland's Hotel. Collins was just as startled to see the priest.

When Father MacAulay asked him what he was doing there, Collins said he had left the rectory because of something Miss MacAulay had said to him. The priest told Collins that the housekeeper meant well, and all would be well if he returned to the rectory. Collins agreed to accompany MacAulay back to New Ireland. But a couple of hours later, when a farmer was ready to drive the priest home in his wagon, Collins was nowhere to be found.

MacAulay and his driver, James Doyle, arrived at the rectory just before six in the evening. There was no sign of

Mary Ann. Oddly, there were dirty dishes and the remains of a meal on the table. It was uncharacteristic of Mary Ann to leave a mess. MacAulay called out, but got no response.

MacAulay looked in the stable and found his horse half-harnessed. He told Doyle to check with the neighbours. If Mary Ann wasn't at any of their houses, he was to ask a young woman named Kate Duffy to come over and make his supper.

Doyle's trip down the road took over an hour. When he returned with Kate, MacAulay was in front of the rectory, pacing back and forth, clearly agitated. He took them inside to witness what he had found.

The priest's office was in a shambles, with papers scattered everywhere. A closet at the foot of the stairs had been broken into. In MacAulay's upstairs bedroom, the closet door had been stove in, likely with an axe. A box containing some money was untouched, but several shirts and other articles of clothing were missing, as well as two valises. Mary Ann's bedroom had also been torn apart. Among several missing items was her gold watch.

MacAulay immediately suspected that Collins had robbed them and then run away. That would explain why he was in Elgin and why he didn't appear for the ride home. Still expecting that Mary Ann would show up sooner or later, he told Kate to make supper.

Kate needed kindling to start a fire in the stove. By now it was dusk, so Doyle went to the woodshed with her to hold a lamp while she gathered up sticks. When they entered the shed, they saw something that froze them in their tracks. Doyle shouted for Father MacAulay to come at once.

Mary Ann was sprawled on the dirt floor as though she had been tossed there like a rag doll. Her face was partially covered by a blood-stained feed sack. Her throat had been slashed from ear to ear. The back of her skull had been cleaved to the brain. Overcome by the sight, MacAulay gasped, "Let me out of this," and ran from the shed. Doyle didn't touch the body because, as he said later, "I smelt the death smell."

Father MacAulay wrote a letter for Doyle to take to the telegraph office at Petitcodiac. From there, the message would be sent to the police in St. John. Besides the report of murder, it named Thomas Collins as the suspect and gave his description. As he drove along the dark road, Doyle stopped to tell neighbours the sensational news.

The next morning, the local coroner, Dr. Suther Murray, arrived at the rectory. News had spread quickly and a small crowd of people had gathered. After examining the body, Dr. Murray enlisted a few onlookers as a coroner's jury. They reached an official verdict: "That the said Miss Mary Ann MacAulay was . . . murdered, that her throat was cut with a knife in the hands of some person unknown, but we believe that person is Thomas J. (sic) Collins, foreigner."

Constables were soon scouring the countryside in search of Collins. At Garland's Hotel, they found a valise full of clothes that he'd left behind. They belonged to Father MacAulay. The officers spoke to many people who had met a man fitting Collins' description. For a supposed murderer fleeing the scene of his crime, Collins didn't seem to be in a great hurry, and he wasn't making any effort to hide.

While women in New Ireland were preparing Mary Ann MacAulay's body for burial, Collins was making his way to St. John. He rode farmers' wagons and had meals with hospitable families. He did a few hours work for pay for one farmer, and at Spruce Lake bought a round of beer for two men who had given him a ride on a lumber wagon. Collins seemed unaware that the newspapers had named him as a murder suspect.

St. John police chief W. Walter Clark sent out instructions for train stations, ports, and border crossings to Maine to be watched. Then he telephoned hotels in St. John and nearby communities, advising the proprietors to be on the lookout for the fugitive. On August 24, 1906, Clark had a call from William Dean, owner of Dean's Hotel in Musquash, fifteen miles west of St. John. A man who looked like Collins was there.

Dean was talking into the phone loudly. Clark told him to lower his voice and to try to keep the suspect there. But Collins evidently overheard Dean and realized he was the subject of the conversation. He quietly slipped away, leaving behind the other valise he'd taken from Father MacAulay's room.

Chief Clark and Detective Patrick Killen drove to Musquash in a carriage. By the time they reached Dean's Hotel, Collins was long gone. However, they learned that the wanted man was heading for St. George. Killen set off in pursuit in the carriage while Clark took a train to head him off.

The next day, Killen caught up to the suspect. Collins tried to flee into the woods but stopped when the detective fired a rifle shot into the air. Collins was exhausted, starving, and suffering from blistered feet.

On the train to St. John, Collins told Clark and Killen that he liked Father MacAulay but couldn't seem to please Miss MacAulay. He said he decided to leave the rectory after she accused him of stealing a can of milk and called him a thief and a liar. "It made me mad," he said.

Collins seemed genuinely stunned when informed that he was being charged with the murder of Mary Ann. He said that on the night of August 19, 1906, he and Miss Macaulay had retired to their rooms at nine o'clock. He lay awake on his cot until he was sure she was asleep. Then he quietly crept into Father MacAulay's bedroom, packed some clothing into the two valises, and returned to his room.

At six the next morning, Miss MacAulay made him breakfast and then told him to hitch the horse to the carriage because she was going out. He hadn't finished harnessing the horse when she came to the stable and said she wasn't going out after all because it was too hot. Then she headed off to a spring in the woods to get water. Collins said he took the opportunity to grab the valises and leave. He admitted to the theft of clothing but denied ransacking the house. Collins swore that when he took his leave of the rectory, Miss MacAulay was alive and well.

In the St. John jail, Father MacAulay identified the prisoner. Collins was then taken by train and wagon to Hopewell Cape, the administrative seat of Albert County, where the trial would be held. All along the way, people gathered to get a look at the now notorious murder suspect. In Hopewell Cape, Collins was formally arraigned on a charge of first degree murder.

All of the evidence connecting Collins to the murder was circumstantial. Marks in the dirt indicated that Mary Ann had not been killed in the woodshed, but that her body had been dragged there. Investigators speculated that Collins killed her when she caught him robbing the house. But they found no blood on the floors or walls. Nor, in spite of an intense search, could they find the axe that had been used to cleave her skull. Mary Ann's throat could have been cut with a razor, and Collins owned one. But so did most men. There were no bloodstains on Collins' clothing. An old pair of Father MacAulay's trousers found in the woodshed had evidently been used to wipe blood off some object.

Some of the people who claimed to have met a man who looked like Collins in the days following the murder said he had a gold watch. However, when Collins was arrested, the only watch in his possession was a silver one. Could the stranger with the gold watch have been someone else? Mary Ann's missing watch never turned up.

Then there was that earlier burglary at the rectory. Could the thief who stole the whiskey and wine have come back and been surprised by Mary Ann while ransacking the house? An assault and robbery committed against a pedlar in the vicinity within a day or so of the murder made that a possibility.

While many people were certain of Collins' guilt, others had doubts. They thought such a boyish face couldn't possibly hide the deranged mind of a murderer. Word got out that while he sat in his cell, Collins voraciously read every newspaper, magazine, and book he could get. That didn't seem to fit the image of an uneducated lout from a Liverpool slum. Then the newspapers reported that Premier Lemuel J. Tweedie was going to assume the role of attorney general and represent the Crown against Collins. Tweedie's involvement, although short-lived, was the first time a New Brunswick premier personally prosecuted a case. It appeared that the government was determined to get a conviction in what was fast becoming a very high-profile case. To his many sympathizers, Collins was being railroaded on the premise that he must have done it because the police didn't have any other suspects. Those who questioned Collins' guilt, or at least the manner in which justice was being administered, took up a collection to pay for his defence counsel.

The judicial proceedings started with a preliminary hearing in September 1906, and went through three trials, with the last one ending on September 24, 1907. It would be one of the most controversial courtroom dramas in New Brunswick history. There were difficulties in jury selections because most potential jurors had made up their minds about the defendant's guilt or innocence, or questioned the morality of capital punishment.

The prosecution dropped a bombshell when, 129 days after the crime, it suddenly produced the murder weapon — the long-missing axe. A seventeen-year-old girl named Mabel Williamson whom Father MacAulay had employed as a housemaid said she'd found it in his bedroom. It was leaning against the wall behind his commode.

Collins' lawyers, Harrison McKeown and J.C. Sherren, thought it incredulous that police could have failed to find the axe if it had been there all along. Detective Killen, who'd been in charge of the search, said he'd have given anything to be the one to find it.

Dr. G. Addy, a St. John pathologist who examined the axe, said it had dried blood on it, but couldn't swear the blood was human. McKeown pointed out that if the axe with fresh blood on it had been placed behind the commode right after the murder, there would be bloodstains on the floor and on the "splasher," a cotton sheet behind the commode that protected the wallpaper. There were no such stains.

In the absence of eyewitnesses, the Crown's case relied on a long list of people who claimed to have encountered Collins, or someone they thought was him, as he travelled from New Ireland to St. John. Defence counsel had letters from people in Liverpool attesting to Collins' good character. There was no evidence that he had ever been in trouble with the law.

In the midst of the proceedings, Father MacAulay suffered a heart attack on February 3, 1907, while preparing for Sunday mass, and died. Dr. Murray said the strain of the murder and the trial had been too much for him. Father MacAulay was buried next to Mary Ann in the St. Agatha churchyard.

The first trial ended with a guilty verdict. McKeown immediately requested a "Crown reserve" (equivalent of a mistrial) on the grounds that the judge, Mr. Justice Gregory, had committed technical errors in his instructions to the jury. Gregory denied the errors and sentenced Collins to hang. But the trial transcripts supported McKeown, and the Supreme Court of New Brunswick granted Collins a new trial.

The same evidence was examined, the same people questioned. This time the result was a hung jury. The jurors stood at seven to five in favour of acquittal, with no hope of a unanimous decision.

The final trial marked the first time in Canada that a defendant was tried three times on the same murder charge. Having won over more than half the jurors in the second trial, McKeown might have had high hopes for an acquittal. But by now the public had grown weary of the case. Spectators no longer packed the courtroom. It was harvest time, and witnesses and jurors were anxious to get back to their fields. To speed things along, Mr. Justice Hanington started court early in the day and allowed sessions go well into the evening.

When all the testimony had been given, McKeown made an eloquent plea. However, the jury reached a unanimous verdict of guilty. Collins showed no emotion when Hanington sentenced him to hang on November 15, 1907.

Over a thousand of Collins' sympathizers signed a petition to have the death sentence commuted to life imprisonment. But the federal government wouldn't grant clemency. An attempt to have Collins declared insane also failed.

Radclive the hangman arrived in Hopewell to carry out the execution. At his own request, Collins did not die in the dark hour just after midnight, but in the light of dawn.

His body was buried in an unmarked grave in the jail yard, where his bones would be discovered sixty years later.

Newspapers reported that near the end, Collins confessed to his priest that he had killed Mary Ann when she caught him robbing the house. But no source for this "confession" was ever determined. All who were with Collins in his last hours, including his spiritual advisors, denied that he had admitted to the crime.

The murder of Mary Ann MacAulay had been officially avenged. But for many years wild rumours circulated. In one story, Mary Ann revealed to Father MacAulay that she was pregnant with his child. The priest had her killed and then framed Collins. In another yarn, Mary Ann caught Father MacAulay and Collins in bed together and Father MacAulay had her killed to silence her.

Some people couldn't dismiss the possibility that an unknown intruder was the killer, and Collins had the bad luck to be in the wrong place at the wrong time. He also picked the worst possible moment to become a thief. *Maybe* Thomas Collins *did* kill Mary Ann. But when the law demands that guilt be established beyond the shadow of a doubt, *maybe* shouldn't be enough to send the accused to the gallows.

10

Cape Breton: A Trio of Murders

The Koziel Murder: A Stranger in the Woods
On May 18, 1914, the people of the village of Birch Grove, Nova Scotia, just south of Glace Bay, were alarmed to learn that a child had been abducted. Six-year-old Elzbieta Koziel and her brother had been sent to fetch a pail of water from a stream a short distance behind their house. The little boy returned home alone. He told his parents that a strange man had stopped them and then carried Elzbieta into the woods. He said his sister kicked and screamed, but the man put his hand over her mouth.

The news spread quickly, and soon search parties were combing the woods. They found Elzbieta's partially nude body in the stream in a marshy area. Her clothing lay scattered nearby.

Albert and Mary Koziel and their children were Polish immigrants. They had been in Cape Breton less than a year. In the newspaper accounts of their daughter's abduction and murder, Elzbieta would be known by the English version of her name, Elizabeth. The brother who had witnessed the attack wouldn't be named at all. Census records show that Elizabeth had a brother named Albert who would have been about ten at the time.

Special Agent D.A. Noble of the Nova Scotia Steel and Coal Company police organized a search for Elizabeth's killer. His men found a transient walking along the railway tracks near the crime scene. The man somewhat matched the description Albert had given of the stranger: young, of medium size, and wearing faded old clothes. But hundreds of men could have fit that description, so the suspect was arrested on a technical charge of trespassing on railway property and taken to the Glace Bay jail for questioning.

As it turned out, this man was a Newfoundlander who had been on his way from Sydney to Birch Grove when he encountered the posse. Noble released the man when he proved he was in Sydney at the time of Elizabeth's abduction. Nonetheless, the Newfoundlander was probably fortunate that he'd been picked up by Noble's men. Elizabeth's grief-stricken father was roaming the woods and the railway line with a shotgun, looking for his daughter's killer.

The eyewitness account of a young boy didn't give Noble much to go on. Then two Birch Grove women reported that they had seen a man near the crime scene. The description they provided matched the one Albert had given, but with more details. It fit a miner named Gustave Brauer. At one o'clock in the afternoon on May 19, 1914, Noble's constables found Brauer working his shift in a Glace Bay mine and arrested him there.

Brauer was a twenty-year-old German Pole who had arrived in Cape Breton five years earlier. He spoke fluent English, and according to the *Sydney Post*, appeared "intelligent." He denied any involvement with the crime when Noble questioned him in the Glace Bay jail. However, his work boots were covered with the same kind of mud found in the marsh where Elizabeth had been murdered and his undershirt was spotted with what appeared to be dried blood. A search of the shack he lived in turned up a shirt that also had stains that seemed to be blood, and a pair of pants that were caked up to the knees with marsh mud.

The evidence was circumstantial, and Noble advised Brauer that anything he said would be written down and used later in court. In the absence of any legal counsel, Brauer confessed to the abduction and murder. The *Post* reported, "He told the details of his crime . . . minutely, and did not appear to be a trifle nervous or embarrassed . . . He was perfectly cool at all times and told his blood-curdling story vividly, leaving nothing, apparently, out."

In the presence of witnesses, Brauer told Noble that on the evening of May 18, 1914, he had joined shocked and saddened neighbours in the Koziel home where the victim's body lay in view, and where the mother was incapacitated with grief. He thought that would "throw the authorities off his scent." The next morning he'd gone to work as usual and didn't know the police suspected him until his boss ordered him to the surface. Curiously, Brauer also told Noble that in his home country, people found guilty of such crimes were sometimes hanged or sentenced to long prison terms, but often got off light with just four or five years.

The editors of the *Post* had high praise for the swift manner in which Special Agent Noble had apprehended the killer. Readers were reminded that three years earlier, Noble had apprehended an American fugitive named Frank Hollis who was wanted for murder in New Jersey. With Brauer, a confessed murderer, behind bars, the *Post* hailed Noble and his men as "a force which is rapidly coming to the front as being one of the most effective police organizations in the country."

But even as Noble was being commended as a police hero, he had to turn his attention to protecting the man he had just arrested. "Owing to the revolting nature of the crime," said the *Post*, "the residents of the colliery district are in a dangerous mood." Hundreds of angry people crowded around the Glace Bay jail. One man shouted, "Lynch him!" Others took up the cry, and it was feared that they might try to rush the jail. However, Noble and his officers faced them down. The crowd dispersed, leaving only a few of the morbidly curious who hoped to get a glimpse of the prisoner.

Brauer's trial was held in late June. Because he had confessed, there was no doubt of his guilt. However, his attorney D.A. Cameron, K.C., one of the foremost criminal lawyers in Nova Scotia, put forth the defence that Brauer was insane and therefore not responsible for his actions. He further argued that the killing had not been intentional. Cameron said that in covering Elizabeth's face with his hand to stifle her screams, Brauer had accidentally smothered her.

The evidence given by Dr. Roy, a local physician who

had done the autopsy, didn't support that possibility. He said the girl's body showed obvious marks of strangulation. Dr. Roy further testified that while Elizabeth had not been "ravished," an attempt had definitely been made.

The spectators in the courtroom included Brauer's mother and a number of people from the German community, some of whom did not speak English. Interpreters translated the proceedings for them. Elizabeth's father was also present.

The jury learned that as a child in Germany, Brauer had fallen from a tree and suffered a head injury that left him mentally unbalanced. He'd been prone to "fits" during which he exhibited vicious behaviour and would torture birds and small animals. For these irrational acts, Brauer's mother would beat him. Cameron argued that Brauer had been seized by such a fit when he attacked Elizabeth.

The story of Brauer's childhood accident and subsequent mental instability earned a degree of sympathy for him among the spectators, especially the German immigrants. The burning question was to what extent Brauer's past would influence the twelve local men who made up the jury?

Weighing against the insanity plea was the testimony of Noble and the other witnesses to Brauer's confession. They said that he appeared to be completely in control of his faculties at the time, and had even been clever enough to try to trick the police by visiting the home of the bereaved family. The prosecution also put young Albert on the witness stand to tell the jury what had happened that terrible day. He pointed to Brauer as the man who had carried off his sister. When the presiding judge, Chief Justice Townsend, asked Albert if he knew where he would go if he told a lie, the boy replied that he would go to hell. Through it all, the jury could see Elizabeth's father, a stricken man expecting hard justice for his child.

When all the witnesses had given their evidence and been cross-examined, the judge left it to the jury to decide whether or not Brauer had been insane at the time of the murder. He instructed them to return with a verdict of guilty or guilty but insane. The jury then retired to deliberate. They weren't out for long.

After just forty minutes, the jury returned and the foreman announced that they had reached a unanimous verdict — guilty. As reported in the *Post*, Chief Justice Townsend addressed the prisoner, giving instructions that his words be translated for the benefit of the Germans.

"Gustave Brauer, you have been given a full and fair trial on the charge of murder of this little girl, and you have been ably defended by your counsel, Mr. Cameron. You have been found guilty of a most fiendish murder and I would advise you to make your peace with your God. The sentence of this court is that you be taken from hence to the county jail and that on Wednesday, the sixteenth day of September next, you be taken to the place of execution and there be hanged by the neck until you are dead. May God have mercy on your soul."

When Townsend's sentence was translated for Brauer's mother, she shrieked and tried to get to her son but was held back. Brauer swooned and then collapsed to the floor. A shudder of surprise ran through the German contingent in the room. They had been certain that Brauer would be found guilty but insane. Elizabeth's father didn't say a word. The *Post* reported that, "he gave a deep sigh as of horror or surprise when he learned of the convicted man's fate."

Brauer was taken to the county jail in Sydney to await his date with the hangman. Cameron sought a reprieve on the grounds that the court had not satisfactorily explored the possibility that Brauer had committed the crime while in a fit of insanity. The lawyer had written to Germany for supporting medical evidence. On September 15, 1914, he was granted a stay of execution until November 11.

Brauer spent those weeks in the "condemned cell" of the Sydney jail. A visitor who was unfamiliar with the case wouldn't have suspected that there was anything unusual about the prisoner. In the daytime, he was allowed to mix with the other inmates. At night, a single guard kept watch to discourage any attempt at escape or suicide.

In spite of German medical documentation attesting to Brauer's unstable mental condition, Cameron was unsuccessful in his efforts to have Brauer declared insane and committed to an institution. Early on the morning of November 11, 1914, after being awakened from an apparently sound sleep, Brauer walked calmly and quietly to the gallows. J.H. Holmes, the executioner, strapped his arms and legs, pulled a hood over his face, and placed the noose around his neck. A Salvation Army captain recited the Lord's Prayer. At 6:45 a.m., Holmes sprang the trap door.

Death appeared to be instantaneous, but the body was left suspended for twenty-five minutes before being cut down. Through the intercession of a local clergyman,

Brauer's mother was allowed to take possession of his remains for interment in Sydney's Hardwood Hill Cemetery rather than burial in an unmarked jail yard grave.

It's unlikely that Brauer would be convicted of murder in a modern day Canadian court. The strong evidence that he was not of sound mind, even in the face of his confession, would send him to an institution for the criminally insane. But in 1914, mental illness was an enigma little understood by police, judges, lawmakers, and the general public. An innocent child had been murdered and the law demanded retribution. However, many Cape Bretoners felt that justice had not really been served by Brauer's execution.

The Dunn Murder: Blood on a Doorknob

In the weeks following the execution of Gustave Brauer, news of the war in Europe dominated the front pages of the *Sydney Post*. However, one dramatic headline had nothing to do with the war. There had been another murder in Cape Breton.

At seven o'clock in the evening on December 21, 1914, Adam Ross locked up his jewellery store in North Sydney and walked to his residence on Queen Street. That was the home of Miss Katherine "Cassie" Dunn, age seventy, one of North Sydney's most well-respected citizens. Miss Dunn's father had established the jewellery store, and after his death, she had managed it herself for several years before selling the business to Ross. He had been a boarder in her spacious house ever since.

When Ross arrived home, he noticed the dining

room table had been set for supper, but there was no sign of Miss Dunn. Thinking she had stepped out for a few minutes, perhaps to go to Moulton's General Store, he sat down to wait for her. When after a short while, Miss Dunn didn't appear, Ross became concerned and began to search the house. He checked several rooms, but had not yet looked in the sitting room, when he noticed that the house was getting cold. He decided to go down to the cellar and shovel some coal into the furnace before continuing his search. At the foot of the cellar stairs, Ross found Cassie Dunn.

The old woman was slumped in a kneeling position, unmoving and unresponsive. The rough floor was covered by a pool of blood that had oozed from an ugly gash in her head. Next to her lay a bloodstained axe. Horrified, Ross rushed up the stairs and immediately summoned Miss Dunn's physician, Dr. Rindress. Because Miss Dunn was kneeling, Ross thought she might still be alive.

Dr. Rindress responded quickly, but pronounced Miss Dunn dead. Her skull had been crushed by several blows. The bloody axe told the story — she had been murdered. Dr. Rindress notified the Sydney police.

As Miss Dunn's body was taken to Dooley's funeral home in North Sydney, the Sydney police began their investigation. They thought at first that Miss Dunn had been the victim of a robbery gone terribly wrong because it appeared that someone had tried, unsuccessfully, to remove a valuable bracelet from her wrist. But if robbery was the motive, why hadn't the killer stolen her rather substantial collection of jewellery?

Near the axe on the cellar floor, the police found a short piece of lead pipe with blood and hair stuck to it. When they looked in the sitting room, they saw blood on the floor and signs of a struggle. It appeared that Miss Dunn's assailant had attacked her in the sitting room, knocked her unconscious with the lead pipe, and then carried her to the cellar where he bashed her skull in with the axe. Bloody fingerprints on the doorknob showed that he had left by the front entrance. The back door was locked.

The officers questioned neighbours, hoping someone might have seen or heard something. A thirteen-year-old girl named Christine Kelly, who often ran errands for Miss Dunn, said that she had been at the house at around three thirty that afternoon and had told Miss Dunn she'd come back later. She returned at five o'clock and was met at the gate by a "coloured man" named John West.

Christine said that West, who evidently had just come out of the house, was pulling on his gloves and had two packages under his arm. He spoke "crossly" to her, Christine said, and warned her not to go into the house. She ran to the other side of the street because West frightened her.

John West, age forty-seven, came from Halifax County and had been in Cape Breton about two years. He was known in various communities on the island because he moved from one place to the other doing whatever jobs he could find. He wasn't a big man, standing just five foot four and weighing about 130 pounds. Strong enough, though, to overpower a seventy-year-old woman! West was a boarder in a house (owned by William Connolly) that was directly across the street from Miss Dunn's house. It was common knowledge in the neighbourhood that boarders in the Connolly house, which lacked plumbing, crossed the road to Miss Dunn's house to fetch pails of water.

Chief MacNeil of the Sydney police department went to Connolly's house and found West at home. MacNeil took West into custody as a suspect and held him in the Sydney jail. The following day, West was taken to Dooley's funeral home where Coroner A.R. Forbes held an official inquest.

West denied any involvement in the murder. He was shown the lead pipe and axe, and said he had never seen them before. Under questioning, West carefully described his movements about the time of the murder. He said he had visited Kelly's ship chandlery, the post office, Jackson's market, and Moulton's store where he bought a pound of sugar. He then went home.

Shortly after five o'clock, West continued, he crossed the street to Miss Dunn's for a pail of water. After taking the water back to Connolly's, he went to Moulton's for another pound of sugar. On his way back from Moulton's, he saw Christine Kelly at Miss Dunn's gate and advised her not to go into the house.

Asked why he had done that, West said that earlier he had seen another "coloured man" enter Miss Dunn's house. He told Forbes, "I saw the little girl steering as if she was going into the gate. I was afraid for her to go in when there was a man in there. I was very nervous and told her she had better not go in."

West also expressed his fear that if Christine saw that other man come out of the house, she might mistakenly report the man as *him*, and he would be arrested. West said he was too far away to recognize the man he had seen entering Miss Dunn's house, but thought he was big enough to be Fred Willis, another of the Connolly house boarders.

Some of West's testimony was puzzling. He said he had been coming from Moulton's when he met Christine Kelly at the gate, but she had said it appeared that he'd just come out of the house. Why would the presence of a man in Miss Dunn's house cause him to fear for Christine's safety? If he thought the man was up to no good, should he not also have been concerned for Miss Dunn? What did he think had happened in the house that could lead to his arrest in a case of mistaken identity? It also seemed odd that he would go back to Moulton's for a second pound of sugar. The coroner's inquest would have to sit for a second session to get some answers. Meanwhile, Chief MacNeil drove to the town of Sydney Mines where Alfred Willis was employed as a painter and whitewasher. He took him into custody as a murder suspect. Willis was lodged in the Sydney jail in a cell separate from John West.

The inquest continued the following day before a coroner's jury. Willis stated that he was a distant cousin of William Connolly's from Guysborough, Nova Scotia, and was a boarder in the Connolly house. However, he had moved in only a week before the murder, following a breakup with his wife. He swore that he had never even set eyes on Miss Dunn. Willis admitted that he'd been arrested a few times for public drunkenness, but otherwise had not been in any kind of trouble with the police.

Willis testified that on the day of the murder he left for

work early in the morning, and was in Sydney Mines until quitting time that afternoon. He caught the five o'clock trolley car to North Sydney, and got off at the Regent Street stop. He walked straight to his boarding house, arriving there at about five thirty. Only Mrs. Connolly and her children were home at the time. William Connolly and John West came in later. They all had supper together and nobody left the house until the police came and arrested West. The Connollys corroborated Willis's story.

The inquest was recessed for Christmas, and the suspects West and Willis spent the holiday in the Sydney jail. A Sydney police detective named Edwards was engaged by the Crown to conduct a thorough investigation. This was in response to an accusation by the *North Sydney Herald* that the Crown had been less than diligent in its efforts to secure evidence.

The coroner's inquest reconvened on December 29, 1914 in the North Sydney courthouse. By this time, the case had aroused so much public interest that spectators filled the room to capacity. The hearings would go on for more than a week, and observers would witness one of the most unusual courtroom dramas in Cape Breton history.

John West's recollection of events had changed over the Christmas break. He now testified that he had seen both Fred Willis and William Connolly enter Miss Dunn's house, but saw only Willis come out. West said that he now remembered seeing Willis in possession of a piece of lead pipe just like the one found at the murder scene. He also swore that at a dance held in Sydney Mines, he had heard Willis utter derogatory remarks about white people.

Willis denied ever making such remarks, and he insisted that he had never carried around a lead pipe. Connolly swore that he had been at work at the time of the murder and said he had witnesses who would support his alibi. Nonetheless, he was placed under arrest and held as a suspect.

As the questioning dragged on, inconsistencies kept cropping up in West's testimony. The route he had taken from Moulton's store changed from one telling to the next. He initially said he hadn't been inside Miss Dunn's house but later said he'd had something to eat in her kitchen. He also couldn't explain why he had to go back to the store for a second pound of sugar.

But for all the oddities in West's testimony, the most perplexing question nagging the police, the coroner's jury, and the public, was that of motive. With robbery all but ruled out, what would drive John West, Fred Willis, William Connolly, or anyone else to murder a seventy-year-old woman who was well-liked by everybody in town?

Meanwhile, Detective Edwards had been busy. His enquiries had revealed that John West had a criminal record, having been jailed in Digby, Nova Scotia, for theft. Edwards had taken photographs of the interior of Miss Dunn's house, including the doorknob with the bloody fingerprints. He said he intended to compare the fingerprints in the photographs with those of the three suspects. On January 6, 1915, Edwards told the inquest that he had uncovered other important evidence that he would present at the proper time.

West continued to give contradictory testimony. Then

on January 8, he surprised everyone in the courtroom when he suddenly asked Coroner Forbes if he could speak to him privately. That was not at all in keeping with regular legal procedure, but Forbes agreed to it.

Behind closed doors, with Detective Edwards as witness, Forbes advised West that anything he said would be taken down in writing to be used as evidence. West said he wanted to confess to the murder of Cassie Dunn. He said he'd been on the verge of admitting his guilt several times during the inquest, but had been afraid he would be dragged out of the courtroom and lynched. "Now I just want you to save me from the gallows," he said to Edwards. "I don't mind a term in the penitentiary, but I don't want to hang, for I am not ready to die."

This statement, which appeared in the *Sydney Post*, has the suspicious ring of editing by a newspaper writer with a flair for the dramatic. There was irony to West asking for Edwards' protection, because it was undoubtedly the detective's work that had resulted in West's confession. Most people were still not very familiar with the use of fingerprinting in criminal investigations. West had probably never heard of it, and would have been startled when Edwards said he had photographed the prints on the doorknob. Then there was the evidence Edwards had said he would present "at the proper time." West had no idea what that evidence might be. His only option was to confess and hope that by so doing he would escape the hangman's rope.

Back in the courtroom, West described what had really happened on December 21, 1914. Mrs. Connolly had sent him to Moulton's to buy sugar and meat. When he was on his way home, he suddenly "conceived the idea of committing rape on Miss Dunn." At those words, a stunned hush fell over the courtroom.

West went to Miss Dunn's house and put his parcels under the front step before opening the door and entering. He found Cassie in the dining room, laying out the table for supper. Neighbours often entered each other's homes without knocking, so she wasn't alarmed. West had been to her house many times to get water. He asked for something to eat, so Miss Dunn prepared a snack for him. While he sat down to eat it, she went into the sitting room.

West finished his meal and then crept into the sitting room, coming up on his victim from behind. He wrapped one arm around her neck, seized her leg with his other hand, and attempted to throw her to the floor. Cassie tried to fight back and scratched West's arm. He smashed her on the nose with his fist, causing a spray of blood that covered his hand. The old woman still resisted, so West pulled the lead pipe from his pocket and struck her on the head, knocking her unconscious.

West then dragged Cassie down the steps to the cellar. He had no thoughts now of sexual assault, only of how to avoid arrest. West was alarmed to see that Miss Dunn was not only still alive, but regaining consciousness. She managed to get up on her knees. West picked up the axe that was already in the cellar and used it to crush Cassie's skull.

West left the house in a hurry, forgetting to pick up the lead pipe. Outside, he noticed that he had blood on his hands, and pulled on his gloves. He didn't realize that he had left gory red fingerprints on the inside doorknob. He retrieved his parcels and was heading down the front walk when Christine Kelly arrived at the gate. He scared her off with a warning not to go into the house, and then walked to the shore to wash the blood off his hands. West returned to the boarding house and gave Mrs. Connolly the parcels. He thought he had gotten away with murder until Chief MacNeil came to the door.

Before West told his gruesome story, Coroner Forbes had warned the spectators that any attempt to interfere with the prisoner would be dealt with promptly. If necessary, he would summon soldiers to assist the police. When West had finished speaking, there was no rush of angry citizens to seize him, no cry for vigilante justice. The revelation that seventy-year-old Cassie Dunn had been murdered while trying to defend herself from a rapist left the people in stunned silence.

One more witness was called upon to give evidence. William Connolly's young son told the inquest that on the night before the murder, West had told him to get some matches from his coat pocket so he could light his pipe. When the boy rummaged through the pockets looking for matches, he found a short piece of lead pipe. He asked West why he had it, and West replied that he intended to sell it.

The other evidence that Detective Edwards had referred to was an article of West's clothing that he had found in the Connolly house. It was a jumper (a type of pullover sweater) that had what appeared to be bloodstains on it. Edwards had taken it to Halifax to be examined in a laboratory. He was still awaiting the results when West made his startling confession.

John West's trial for murder took place shortly after the coroner's inquest. West's hope that his confession would result in a prison sentence was dashed when the jury found him guilty with no recommendation for clemency. The judge sentenced him to be hanged on April 19, 1915. There was little public sympathy for the condemned man because he was, in the words of a *Post* editor, "hopelessly degenerate," and had tried to implicate two innocent men in his crime.

West was sullen as the day of his execution approached. "Since his incarceration in the condemned prisoner's cage," said the *Post*, "West's spiritual requirements have been in the hands of a coloured pastor from Halifax." A rumour circulated that West had told his guards that they would have to carry him to the gallows because he would not walk there.

Whether or not the rumour was true, on April 20, amidst stories of fierce fighting on the Western Front, the *Post* announced, "Confessed Murderer Went To Death Without Faltering." West's only complaint to hangman Holmes as he stood on the scaffold was that the straps on his arms were uncomfortably tight. Holmes loosened them a little. With the noose around his neck and the black hood over his face, West "straightened himself out to his full height and threw out his chest as if entirely prepared for his fate and ready to meet it."

Holmes sprang the trapdoor at 6:23 a.m. The *Post* reported that death was instantaneous. A local Salvation Army captain named Galloway prevailed upon authorities to allow West's body to be buried in Hardwood Hill Cemetery instead of the jail yard. He conducted a graveside funeral that was attended by a few of West's friends. Reports of bloody battles in Europe still filled newspaper pages, but in Cape Breton, for a moment, they gave way to a bizarre case of murder that was solved because of a bloodstained doorknob.

The Brailsford Mystery: Murder or Suicide?

To those who knew her, twenty-two-year-old Edith Mary "Edie" Brailsford was "a girl of prepossessing appearance." Charles Higginbotham would certainly have agreed. Edie had become his fiancée in their hometown of Sheffield, England, before he immigrated to Nova Scotia early in 1921. Higginbotham was a coal miner who'd found himself unemployed due to the recessions and strikes that shook Britain after the Great War. Like many of his colleagues, he'd crossed the Atlantic to work in the Cape Breton coal mines. Higginbotham settled in the town of Dominion, and then paid Edie's passage so she could follow him. She stepped off the White Star liner the SS *Megantic* in Halifax on December 4, 1921, and took the train to Cape Breton. When she arrived in Dominion, her fiancé was overjoyed to see her. But the wedded bliss they had dreamed of back in Sheffield would never be.

Because Edie and Charles were not yet married, it would have been considered scandalous for them to live together. They would also have had financial concerns to overcome before tying the knot and setting up housekeeping. Charles had a job, but Cape Breton had been experiencing the same sort of economic and labour strife he had known in Britain. Miners' wages were low.

Like so many young working class women of the time, Edie "went into service." She became a domestic servant in the home of one of Dominion's more prosperous families. In return for doing housework, she got room and board, plus a small wage. In time, if Edie and Charles were very careful with their money, they eventually could afford to get married.

Dominion was a small community in which everybody knew everybody else, and neighbours frequently visited each other's homes. Once, on a visit to the home of Mackenzie and Susan White, Edie met a young man named John Doucette, Susan's brother. Doucette was from Little Bras d'Or and of Nova Scotian–Acadian background. He resided just down the street at the home of another sister, Mary, and her husband George Fortune.

Edie must have seen something in John Doucette that she didn't see in Charles Higginbotham. In the summer of 1923, she broke off her engagement with Higginbotham and became Doucette's fiancée. There is no record of how Higginbotham took this rejection, but the situation was undoubtedly grist for the town's gossip mills. For Higginbotham, public discourse over the loss of his fiancée to another man would have been humiliating. However, Edie might well have been perceived as ungrateful and fickle for dumping her betrothed, especially after he had paid her passage to Canada. It wasn't long after Edie told Charles she had fallen in love with Doucette that tragedy struck.

On Friday, November 23, 1923, the family with whom Edie lived left for a trip to New Brunswick. Edie didn't want to be in the house alone, so she arranged to stay a night or two with George and Mary. John would be there, so they'd be able to spend some time together. But lately it seemed that their relationship was strained — or so people would say later.

George and Mary lived in a two-storey, four-room house. On the ground floor, the sitting room was at the front and the kitchen at the back. Upstairs were two bedrooms: one for George and Mary and their children and the other for John. The house didn't have electricity, so oil lamps were used after sundown. Cooking was done on a coal-burning iron stove. The sitting room was probably heated by a pot-bellied stove and maybe a fireplace.

Edie arrived at four o'clock in the afternoon. She had supper with John and the Fortune family, and afterwards helped Mary wash the dishes. Then a letter addressed to Edie was delivered to the house. Who sent it and what it said would never be known to anyone but Edie. She read the letter in the kitchen and then burned it in the stove. She said nothing to anyone about what was in the letter. But the manner in which she so quickly destroyed it must have had the others thinking that something odd was going on with Edie.

John and Edie went into the sitting room. Only then did he notice that she had been crying. When John asked her what was wrong, Edie replied, "Nothing!"

From this point, it became apparent that all was not well with John and Edie's relationship. John wanted to take Edie to his sister Susan's house for a visit. Edie didn't want to go because Charles Higginbotham would be there, and she didn't want to see him. She might also have suspected that

John wanted to show her off in front of Charles. John had a tendency to be possessive and boastful, and Edie didn't like that. She would stand up to him if she felt he was getting out of line.

Edie suddenly asked John if he knew a man named Fred Yates and whether or not he was married. With a tone of contempt, John replied that he did know Fred Yates and that Yates was in fact married. Then he derisively asked Edie "if that was the kind of fellow she went out to meet."

Edie icily asked John if that was any of his business. John replied, "It would be my business." Then he put on his coat as though he intended to go to Susan's house whether Edie went with him or not. But instead of going out the door, John went upstairs to his room.

Meanwhile, Mary was still in the kitchen. George had gone upstairs to put the children to bed. He'd decided to lie down on his own bed for a little after-supper repose, but was awake and could see into John's room.

Edie called John downstairs and asked him for a photograph she had given him. John said it was among some other pictures in a trunk in his room and went up to look for it. From his bed, George could see John in his room.

Shortly after ten o'clock, Mary came out of the kitchen with a basin of water she was taking up to John's room. She saw Edie in the shadowy illumination of the oil lamp, sitting in a chair. Just minutes earlier, Edie had been in the kitchen, laughing and chatting with Mary. Now she was occupied with writing a letter to her Uncle Tom in England. Mary found John still rummaging through his trunk. She left the basin and went back down to the kitchen, passing by Edie again.

At about ten thirty, a loud noise shook the house. Mary hurried from the kitchen to the sitting room, which was now in darkness. She dashed up the stairs and met George and John at the top. Mary thought that an oil lamp had exploded and immediately feared a fire. But John had the lamp from his room in his hand and there was no fire on the second floor. Strangely, the lamp in the sitting room had been extinguished. No one had heard a word from Edie.

The three descended the stairs together. By the light of John's lamp they saw Edie lying on the floor in a pool of blood. She had been shot in the head. A pistol lay close to the body. Just *how* close would be one of many questions raised during the inquiry into the violent death of Edie Brailsford. They would prove to be frustrating questions for investigators because confusion quickly fell upon the scene of the tragedy. The one certainty was that the gun that killed Edie belonged to John Doucette.

George's first reaction upon seeing the scene was to run to a neighbour's house and call Dr. M.G. Tompkins. Nobody had yet thought of informing the police. But that didn't mean the news didn't reach almost everybody else in Dominion.

In spite of the late hour, word of the shooting spread like wildfire from house to house. When Dr. Tompkins arrived at the Fortune house, eleven neighbours were already there. Some would later give conflicting testimony about what they saw and heard that night.

George told everyone who came to the house that Edie had shot herself. Doucette appeared to be in shock. First he knelt by Edie's body and wept. Then he sat in the kitchen and asked over and over why Edie had done it. Mary was hysterical. Rita Hicks, one of the neighbours, would later testify that she heard Mary cry, "Oh my God, we'll all be arrested and put in jail, and what will become of our little children!"

Another neighbour, Maude Forbes, would claim that she heard Mary say, "John, you are going to be put in jail for this." Maude's sister, Alice Kendall, would testify that she, too, heard Mary tell John that he'd go to jail. It wasn't necessarily an accusation. Mary might have meant that her brother could be held responsible because the gun was his.

According to Rita Hicks, she first heard of the tragedy when Elizabeth "Lizzie" White, Susan's daughter and John and Mary's niece, came to her door. Lizzie allegedly said, "Oh my God! She has done it at last. Edie has shot herself. She and John Doucette were fighting, and she pulled a revolver from his pocket and shot herself." Lizzie would deny most of that statement, saying that she only told Rita that Edie had shot herself.

It was no secret that Doucette owned a revolver and sometimes carried it in his pocket. Under the law of the time, it was illegal for a person to carry a pistol unless there was reasonable cause to fear assault. Cape Breton mining towns could be rough, especially during times of labour strife. But miners didn't walk around armed. Fighting was done with fists, not guns. Why then, did Doucette feel the need to go armed? Was he afraid that somebody might be out to get him?

Dr. Tompkins found the body lying face up, with the legs fully extended and the arms folded across the chest.

There was a bullet hole in the right side of the head and an exit wound on the other side. The doctor believed that death had been instantaneous. While he was conducting his examination, Chief Victor Gouthro of the Dominion police department arrived; someone had finally gotten around to sending for him.

A coroner's inquest was quickly convened. The jury reached an "open verdict" that concluded that the deceased had died violently under suspicious circumstances, but with an undetermined cause — murder or suicide? Chief Gouthro had John Doucette arrested as "apparently the only one possessing both the opportunity and a reasonable motive for committing the crime." In the weeks that followed, Doucette was held in the Sydney jail. The *Sydney Post* speculated that under the "open verdict," Mary Fortune, the last person known to have seen Edie alive, could also be indicted. A warrant was made out for Mary's arrest but was never executed. Preliminary hearings began on December 4, 1923, and ended ten days later with an official decision to try John Doucette for murder.

The Brailsford case is one of the most intriguing mysteries in Cape Breton legal history. Unfortunately, a fire in 1959 destroyed the old Sydney Court House and all of the records stored there. The only accounts that remain of the investigation and trial are those that appeared in the *Post*. They say nothing about such points as who delivered the mysterious letter or what was happening with George and Mary's children during such traumatic events. Nonetheless, the newspaper articles provide a window into the controversy surrounding the raging question: Was it suicide or murder?

Doucette claimed that Edie had "attacks of melancholy." He said that she became jealous when she thought he was spending more time playing cards with his friends than with her, and threatened to poison herself. On one occasion, said Doucette, Edie drank "a light liquid" that made her sick. Whether or not that was an actual suicide attempt (or if it happened at all), the story supported Doucette's claim that Edie was not of sound mind.

Mary Fortune somewhat backed her brother's testimony. She said that Edie was often "gay and jolly," but at other times seemed "sad and depressed." However, aside from Doucette, no one who knew Edie could say that she had ever said anything that would cause them to fear that she would kill herself. One of the strongest pieces of evidence against the suicide theory was the unfinished letter to her Uncle Tom. Edie had written that she wanted to visit him in England and take John with her.

Did Edie kill herself because she had learned she was pregnant? At that time, there was a terrible social stigma attached to pregnancy out of wedlock. Unwed mothers were objects of scorn and were shunned — sometimes by their own families. It wasn't uncommon for women in that predicament to take drastic measures like suicide. An autopsy was performed on Edie's body, but there is no surviving report of her being pregnant at the time of her death.

What was in the letter Edie had burned and who was the author? Did it contain a threat or some form of blackmail that so frightened Edie that she saw death as her only escape? Or did John Doucette feel so threatened by Edie's relationship with Charles Higginbotham, or her possible relationship with Fred Yates, that he killed her in a fit of rage?

If Edie did in fact shoot herself, how she got Doucette's gun is a mystery within a mystery. Could she, as the rumour started by Lizzie White claimed, have pulled it out of Doucette's pocket? That hardly seems likely. Doucette would have had to stand there without resisting while she reached into his pocket for the weapon, and then passively look on while she put it to her head and pulled the trigger.

Doucette admitted that he had the gun in his pocket that night. He said that when he went up to his room to get the photograph she'd asked for, he took the revolver out of his pocket and placed it on the bureau. Doucette's explanation was that while he was busy rummaging through his trunk, Edie must have slipped into the room behind his back and taken the gun. He wouldn't have heard her footsteps because she was in sock feet. Mary testified that Edie had taken off her shoes at suppertime because she had a sore ankle. Mary further said that John couldn't have come down from his room to shoot Edie because he was wearing shoes and she would have heard his footsteps on the stairs.

George testified that he did not think he could have failed to see John leave his room. But he would *not* say that it was impossible for John to go downstairs without being seen by him. No record survives of what George had to say about John's suggestion that Edie crept into his room and took the gun. There was doubt over the reliability of George and Mary's accounts, because they would have been inclined to protect Doucette.

The death scene presented numerous problems, not the least of which was intruding neighbours whose presence hampered the investigation and whose gossip and innuendo would be taken as "evidence" in court. Witnesses couldn't agree on where the gun was located: beside Edie's body or under her arm. At some point before the police arrived, Mary allegedly picked the gun up and handed it to Doucette. Police found a bullet hole in a wall, three-and-a-half feet up from the floor. However, the bullet was never recovered, even after police took the wall apart.

Dr. Tompkins and other witnesses reported seeing blood on John and Mary's hands and clothing, including a bloody handprint on John's shirt. This could easily have resulted from attempts to lift Edie up or cradle her head. Mary might have left the handprint on John's shirt if she held him in a sisterly embrace during the emotion-laden minutes after the discovery of the body. However, there was also blood on the chair Edie had been sitting in, on the table on which she'd been writing her letter, and on a settee in front of the chair. The chair was three feet from where the body lay. That was the principal physical evidence for suspicion of murder, according to Dr. Tompkins.

George insisted that the body had not been moved from the position in which he, his wife, and brother-in-law had found it. But the doctor was certain that it had been moved. The bloodstains on the chair and the location of the bullet hole in the wall indicated that Edie had been sitting when she was shot. The position of the body was not compatible with that. The doctor said that once the bullet pierced Edie's brain, it would have been impossible for her to stand up, stagger a couple of steps, and then collapse and land on the floor in the position in which he saw her: straight out, with arms folded. If Edie had shot herself while sitting in the chair, logic said that her body would have been found in the chair. If she had shot herself while standing a few feet away from the chair, logic said that although the chair, table, and settee might have been sprayed with blood, the bullet hole in the wall would have been higher. There was no doubt, as far as Dr. Tompkins was concerned, that the body had been moved by someone trying to make murder look like suicide.

When John Doucette finally went on trial before Mr. Justice Mellish on February 19, 1924, the Brailsford case had drawn so much publicity that Nova Scotia Deputy Attorney General Angus L. MacDonald had arrived in Sydney to assist Crown Prosecutor Malcolm Patterson, K.C. Leading the defence for Doucette was James W. Maddin, K.C., considered to be one of the best criminal lawyers in Nova Scotia. If he failed in this case, Doucette would hang.

The main witness for the prosecution was Dr. Tompkins, who testified that Edie could not have shot herself, given the position of the body and the locations of the bloodstains and the bullet hole. The prosecution also argued the points that Edie had not left a suicide note and had in fact been writing an optimistic letter to her uncle. There was sworn testimony that Edie and Doucette had quarrelled and that Doucette was in possession of the very weapon with which Edie had supposedly taken her own life. The Crown did its best to convince the jury that Doucette had killed Edie in jealous anger and that he and his sister and brother-in-law had then moved the body and tried to make it appear that she had committed suicide.

Maddin argued that the whole case against Doucette was purely circumstantial. He lambasted witnesses who had spread groundless rumours in the aftermath of the shooting, and who then took the stand in court to give hearsay as evidence. Maddin warned the jury not to convict Doucette on testimony based on "tattle, talebearing, and gossip."

John Doucette, said Maddin, was known to be a man of good character. He had never been in any kind of trouble with the law and neither had his sister or brother-in-law. Maddin further suggested that if Doucette had in fact killed Edie, it would have been easy for him, Mary, and George to have hidden the crime by getting rid of the body. There were plenty of abandoned mine workings, pits, and shafts in the district where a corpse could be tucked away with little chance of ever being found. But nobody had tried to hide the body. George had gone to call for the doctor.

Maddin pointed out that with eleven neighbours crowded into the sitting room before Dr. Tompkins and Chief Gouthro even arrived on the scene, it was entirely possible that furniture had been moved. The position of Edie's body might even have been changed by people who tried to attend to her, not realizing that she was already dead.

The unfinished letter to Edie's uncle and the absence of a suicide note initially seemed damning to Doucette's case. But balanced against them was the mysterious letter she had burned. Something in that letter could have so unhinged her mentally that it resulted in spontaneous suicide.

The Crown couldn't prove that Doucette had shot Edie. It was possible that, unseen by John or George, she had crept into John's room when he was preoccupied, and taken his gun. Then just as stealthily, she could have gone back to the sitting room, extinguished the lamp, and then shot herself.

Justice Mellish surprised everyone in the courtroom when he brought the proceedings to an abrupt halt before all of the witnesses summoned by the Crown had testified. He said that the prosecution's case rested entirely on circumstantial evidence and that the defence had established reasonable doubt of Doucette's guilt. In his instructions to the jury, the judge emphasized that the Crown had failed to produce a solid motive for Doucette to murder Edie. The jury retired and took only fifty-five minutes to reach a unanimous verdict of not guilty.

Doucette stepped out of the prisoner's box a free man. He was immediately surrounded by friends and relatives who embraced and congratulated him. Among the throng were his elderly father and his sister Mary, both of whom kissed him on the cheek.

The late Edie Brailsford had no family in Nova Scotia. Curiously, her fiancé John Doucette was not the informant for her death certificate, which is dated December 24, 1923. The name that appears on the document is that of her jilted fiancé, Charles Higginbotham. Quite likely he was also the person who filled in the names of her parents in England.

Although Charles performed this last official duty on Edie's behalf, he evidently wasn't willing to cover the cost of her funeral as he had been for her passage from England. Nor, it would seem, was John Doucette willing to pay to have his late fiancée's remains laid to rest. Perhaps neither one could afford such an expense. A sad note in the tragedy of Edie Brailsford was a notice that appeared in the *Sydney Post* requesting "the charitable" to donate funds for her funeral and burial. The Brailsford case remains a Cape Breton enigma.

11

Neri and Loder: Two for the Gallows

Secret Evidence

On the morning of June 28, 1917, brothers Fred and Harold Hanes of Evansville, a small community near Stellarton, Nova Scotia, were walking to the MacGregor Pit Mine where they were employed. They took a shortcut along a seldom-used path and came upon a man lying on his back beside the trail. He was bare chested, with his coat wrapped around his head. The brothers thought he was drunk and tried to raise him to wake him up. But to their horror, the man's head almost came off. His throat and neck had been cut nearly all the way through, so that only a strip of flesh attached the head to the body. As Fred and Harold recoiled from the grisly sight, they noticed a revolver on the ground near the man's hand.

The brothers hurried to report their discovery to the local constable, George Davidson, who quickly contacted Stellarton Chief of Police James Watters. When Watters arrived at the scene, he immediately noted that although the victim had practically been decapitated, there wasn't much blood on the ground. The man had been murdered somewhere else and the body dumped by the trail. The revolver was fully loaded but hadn't been fired.

The murdered man was identified as forty-five-year-old Peter Marablito, a miner. He and his forty-three-year-old wife Carmello and a young lodger named Victor Pratti lived in a house just a quarter of a mile from where the body had been found. Watters sent Constable Davidson to the house while Coroner Dr. C.S. Elliott examined the body. Elliott also believed the man had been killed elsewhere.

Nobody was home at the Marablito house. A neighbour told Davidson that Carmello and Pratti were out looking for Peter. Davidson found them in Evansville in the company of twenty-two-year-old Natali Neri who said he was a friend of the family.

When Davidson informed them that Peter Marablito had been found dead, they reacted with shock and surprise. Carmello broke into tears and almost collapsed. Davidson noticed that her face showed signs of weeping *before* he broke the terrible news.

Pratti was the first one Watters questioned. Pratti said that the night before, he had returned home from his shift in the mine at 11:30 p.m. and found Carmello and Neri in an anxious state. Carmello tearfully told him that Peter had gone out at 8:30 p.m. to buy some medicine and hadn't returned. She and Neri were afraid something had happened to him.

Sure that Peter was off drinking somewhere and would

turn up before morning, Pratti went to bed. At 2:30 a.m., Carmello and Neri shook him awake. Peter had still not come home, and they wanted Pratti to help look for him. The three had been going from house to house when Constable Davidson found them. When their turn came to be questioned, Carmello and Neri gave almost identical accounts.

Watters didn't have much to go on. What could have been the motive? A wallet with money in it was still in Marablito's pocket, so Watters ruled out robbery. Was it possible that Marablito was the victim of a love triangle, even though Carmello was twice the age of Pratti and Neri?

Watters began to question the people of Evansville. He learned that Marablito was a friendly, easygoing man whom everybody liked. He sometimes overindulged in wine but was never troublesome. No one Watters spoke to could think of a reason why anyone would want to kill him. When Victor Pratti first arrived from Italy in 1914, Marablito had gotten him a job in the mine, and he and Carmello had taken the young man in as a boarder.

The Marablito home was one half of a double wood-frame company house that was typical of mining communities. The other half was the residence of Alphonse and Eugenia Lemail. Watters learned from them that the Marablitos were childless. Pratti was their only boarder, but Neri was at the house so often that he may as well have lived there.

The Lemails said the Marablitos were good neighbours. They never heard sounds of arguing or anything unusual coming from the other side of the building. When Watters asked if there was any indication that Carmello might be having an affair with one of the young men, they said no. Carmello was in poor health because of a heart ailment, they said. Even if Pratti or Neri had such an interest in a woman her age, she was too frail for such carrying on.

Watters searched the house. He found no evidence of violence and no sign that blood had been scrubbed from floors or walls. He examined all of the clothing on the premises, but nothing was bloodstained. He found an axe and a hatchet, tools that were in almost every household in the community, but there were no traces of blood on them.

However, in a crawl space beneath the kitchen floor, Watters found a mat with tiny bloodstains on it. He had a hunch that Marablito had been killed in the house because of a domestic dispute and Pratti or Neri — or both — had carried the body away and dumped it. The bloodstained mat was slim circumstantial evidence, but Watters arrested Carmello, Pratti, and Neri on suspicion of murder.

In jail, all three repeated the story they'd told Davidson. They insisted they'd known nothing of his death until informed by the police. Carmello said the old mat had been in the crawl space for a long time, and the blood on it was from an animal.

While the suspects awaited trial, Watters interviewed dozens of local residents, looking for any evidence that Carmello and the young men had a reason to want Peter out of the way. By that time, the murder was the main topic of rumours. One woman said she'd seen Carmello and Neri lying on a bed together in Peter's presence. There was another story that Pratti and Neri had been about to bury the body in the woods when they were startled by the sound of a horse. Afraid that someone was nearby, they dropped the body and fled. This story, like the rest of the gossip, had no basis in fact.

With only the bloodstained mat as evidence, Crown Prosecutor Douglas Graham of New Glasgow decided to separate Pratti from the others. He thought that if Pratti saw an opportunity for gaining immunity by giving King's evidence, he would tell the whole story. The general public opinion was that Carmello and at least one of the men were guilty.

In late October, Carmello and Neri stood trial in Pictou before Mr. Justice Russell. To the disappointment of Crown Prosecutor Graham and most of the spectators in the crowded courtroom, Pratti was a letdown as a star witness. He told the same story the three of them had been repeating since the time of the murder.

Graham had no proof that the mat was in any way connected with the crime. He couldn't even prove that the blood on it was human. Any suggestion that Carmello was involved in an illicit relationship with Pratti or Neri was pure hearsay.

Defence Counsel William Macdonald pounced on discrepancies and weaknesses in the prosecution's evidence. He thought the Crown's case so shabby that he didn't even bother to put his clients on the stand. By the time the jury retired to deliberate, Macdonald was certain he had won an acquittal.

However, a brutal murder had been committed, and

somebody had to pay for it. The jury came to the unanimous conclusion that the defendants must have done it because the police hadn't found any other suspects. On October 26, to the astonishment of everyone in the courtroom, they returned a verdict of guilty with a recommendation for mercy.

Under the law of the time, Justice Russell had no choice but to pronounce the death penalty. He sentenced Carmello and Neri to be hanged in the Pictou jail on January 15, 1918. Then he immediately wrote letters to the Minister of Justice and the Secretary of State, recommending that the death penalty he had just handed down be commuted to imprisonment. The judge felt that the jury had reached the wrong verdict.

Waiting in the death cell proved to be more than a woman in Carmello's fragile state of health could endure. She died of a heart attack on Christmas Eve. That backhanded gift from the gods spared her from an appointment with the hangman.

While Neri waited to hear the federal government's decision on his fate, a petition for clemency was circulated. Hundreds of local people signed it, and it was sent to Ottawa. However, a secret document sealed Neri's doom.

Along with the transcripts from the trial, Justice Russell's letters, and the petition, the Department of Justice received written evidence that had not been produced during the trial. On the basis of that document, all pleas on Neri's behalf were dismissed. Macdonald demanded the right to see that evidence but was denied. Protesting his innocence to the very end, Natali Neri was hanged by executioner

Arthur Ellis on the appointed day.

Victor Pratti was released without being prosecuted. Nobody had a satisfactory explanation for the gun found beside Marablito's body. The secret evidence that sent Neri to the gallows remains a mystery to this day.

A Can of Salmon

The Loder brothers of Prince Edward Island just couldn't seem to stay out of jail. George, born in Rustico in 1887, began stealing at an early age. James, four years younger, followed his big brother's example. In 1905, eighteen-year-old George went to prison for stealing horses. At the time of his arrest, he was in possession of a pistol. According to the *Charlottetown Guardian*, George was a "bright looking boy" who seemed perfectly unconcerned about the "grave consequences" that awaited him.

George was out on parole in September 1910, when he, James, and another youth burglarized a store in Stanley Bridge. They were soon tracked down and arrested. The census of 1911 shows George and James both residing in the Dorchester Penitentiary in New Brunswick.

For a few years after his release, George managed to avoid being arrested for anything, while James was in jail more than he was out of it. At some point, George moved to Pictou, where he evidently did honest work as a handyman. He might also have been supplementing his income by less legitimate means at night.

Daniel Barry was one of Pictou's most successful and well-respected residents. He and his brother Alfred operated a gristmill, a sawmill, and an ice house. Barry was elderly and had become somewhat reclusive. After suffering a crippling accident in 1919, he rarely left the big stone house where he lived alone. A housekeeper came by every day to prepare his meals and do chores.

On the morning of December 30, 1920, the housekeeper arrived to find the front door locked. She knocked, and when nobody answered she went to the home of neighbour Thomas Hudson, who immediately telephoned Alfred.

A small crowd soon gathered in front of Barry's house. Alfred arrived and started trying the ground-floor windows. Then someone saw smoke coming from the house.

Firemen arrived within minutes of the alarm being sounded. They broke down the door and rushed in to find a sofa ablaze in the room that was Barry's main living quarters. Barry lay sprawled on the sofa, dead. The firemen extinguished the flames before the body could be consumed.

At first it was thought that Barry had fallen asleep on the sofa while smoking and his pipe had started the fire. But the autopsy revealed that he had been shot. The bullet had pierced his skull behind one ear and travelled down to the collarbone, which indicated that the killer had been standing above and behind him.

Although the body was partially burned, the coroner determined that Barry had been dead for four or five hours before the housekeeper knocked on the door. Fire investigators concluded that the blaze had started just before the people outside saw smoke. Evidence showed that the sofa and the body had been soaked with kerosene. Alfred Barry searched the house and told police that two gold watches and about four hundred dollars were missing; so was the revolver his brother kept in the house for protection.

Pictou Chief of Police D.L. McAuley and Constable D.A. Morrison began the hunt for the murderer. They questioned everyone who might have seen or heard something that could provide a lead. Their first break came with a young man named Daniel Reid who worked for one of Barry's neighbours.

Reid said he had seen a man he knew as George Loder loitering around the Barry house the day before the murder and had even spoken to him. McAuley soon learned that George Loder had a long criminal record. He started digging for any information he could find about Loder's recent activities. By good luck, he discovered that a few hours before Reid saw him, Loder had telephoned the Barry house from nearby Westville. He had been overheard saying that he was going to Pictou to deliver a piece of machinery. Soon after, he arrived in Pictou on the train.

Loder went from the station to John McDonald's grocery store. Among his purchases were two cans of salmon. When Loder left the store, he was headed in the direction of Barry's house.

McDonald, who had personally sold Loder the salmon, was the deputy chief of Pictou's volunteer fire department. He had been one of the first men through the door at the Barry fire. The next day, as part of the investigating team, McDonald found the cans in Barry's room. One can was empty and the other was unopened. McDonald's store carried a brand of canned salmon that was not sold by other grocers in the area. McAuley was now certain that Loder had been in the house.

The police learned that on the evening of December 30, 1920, Loder had been "drinking about town" with two companions. People saw that he had a lot of money and a revolver. They'd also noticed that one leg of his trousers was torn. The following morning, Loder had taken the train to Westville. There, his trail ran cold. No one knew where he had gone.

McAuley contacted Halifax for help, which came in the form of Chief Detective Horace Kennedy. He spoke to everybody who had ever been associated with Loder and had constables comb all of his haunts. He sent Loder's description to police departments all over the Maritimes. He soon got results.

The Pictou police received a wire from Sheriff G.B. McNutt of Prince County, Prince Edward Island, that he had Loder in the Summerside jail. The suspect had been arrested at his sister's home. A constable had taken him by surprise in the early morning while he was still in bed and had no chance to reach for his gun. McAuley and Kennedy went to Summerside to pick the suspect up.

Loder admitted he'd been in Barry's house. He'd been caught with the revolver and the two gold watches, but he denied committing murder.

Loder claimed that weeks earlier he'd done some work for Barry, who agreed to pay him eighty-four dollars. Then Barry had said he didn't have the cash on hand. He told Loder he'd have to wait until he could go to the bank.

After that, said Loder, Barry kept putting him off with

excuses. Finally, Loder telephoned Barry from Westville and asked if he had the money. Barry said yes, and Loder took the train to Pictou. He stopped and bought canned salmon at McDonald's store before going to the house.

Loder said he had a bottle with him and he and Barry got drunk. Then they quarrelled over the money. Barry suddenly pulled a revolver and said, "I'd rather be shot than give you your money."

Loder grabbed the gun, and it discharged in the struggle, killing Barry. Instead of fleeing, Loder ransacked the house, taking the watches and cash. He ate a can of salmon and stayed all night.

In the morning, Loder heard someone at the door. He poured kerosene from a lamp over Barry's body and the sofa and set it alight. Then he went out through a back door. He tore his trousers climbing over the backyard fence. Loder said he stayed in town for a while to throw off suspicion.

McAuley and Kennedy didn't believe Loder's story. They'd found evidence that a back window had been forced open, and the location of the bullet wound didn't support his version of the shooting. It appeared more likely that Loder had broken into the house with robbery in mind. When the physically handicapped Barry confronted him with the revolver, Loder took it from him and shot him.

Loder stood trial for murder before Justice Russell on June 17, 1921. Defence Counsel D.D. McDonald argued that Loder had killed Barry in self-defence after Barry threatened him with a gun. He said that if the jury found

Loder guilty of anything, it should be the lesser charge of manslaughter.

Crown Prosecutor Douglas Graham presented Loder as a cool, calculating criminal who broke into a crippled old man's house in the dead of night. He could easily have disarmed Barry without killing him. But Loder murdered him and then deliberately started a fire to cover his crime. "If we fail to convict the man in the criminal box," Graham told the jury, "we have failed in our duty indeed."

The members of the jury agreed. They found Loder guilty with no recommendation for mercy. Justice Russell sentenced him to hang on August 31.

According to the newspaper report, on the appointed day, Loder was "quite composed and ascended the scaffold without falter. The drop worked successfully, and death was instantaneous." Loder was the last person to be hanged in the Pictou jail and the only murder suspect in Canada whose trip to the gallows was due to a can of salmon.

12

Benny Swim: The Man Who Was Hanged Twice

Hard luck was Benny Swim's constant companion from the day he was born: April 21, 1900. His parents, William and Eva, were among the poorest residents of one of the most impoverished regions of Atlantic Canada. Eva gave birth in a squalid one-room cabin in the woods.

Benny grew up in a part of Carlton County, New Brunswick, that was often called the Badlands. It was a mixture of forest and hardscrabble farms where people lived on the margins of society. Men put meat on the table by hunting, often with little regard for game laws. They earned hard cash by making moonshine in secret stills and selling it for as little as two dollars a gallon.

Poverty, over-proof liquor, and a proliferation of firearms resulted in a high rate of violent crime. Quarrels and domestic disputes often ended in assault and even murder. Among the poorly educated, underemployed, clannish backwoods families, there was a deep mistrust of police and other authority figures and outsiders in general.

Unlike the backwoods boys who were hardened early to a rough-and-tumble life, Benny wasn't a tough kid. He was withdrawn and moody, and had few friends. He hated his home and often fought with his parents. While still very young, he moved in with his uncle, John Swim, who farmed near Rockland.

Benny liked living with his uncle, but he was having trouble at school with bullies who tormented him remorselessly. One day, twelve-year-old Benny came home in a fit of anger and asked what he could do to make the kids leave him alone. Uncle John told him to fight back — with a weapon.

The next day, when the schoolyard bullies began to taunt him, Benny charged at them with a knife. The slashing blade sent the bullies running, and Benny was elated over his victory. But that was his last day at school.

Benny eventually went to work in a pulp mill. He put in long hours for low pay doing one of the dreariest, most back-breaking, bad-smelling jobs in Canada. In a way, the mill seemed representative of Benny Swim's cheerless existence.

An introvert with limited social skills, Benny was awkward around girls. But there was one young woman about whom he developed an obsession. She had long, jet black hair and full, sensuous lips, the most alluring feature of her otherwise rather plain face. She had a strikingly beautiful body, what one observer called, "the build of a Venus." The simple gingham dresses she wore showed off the white skin of her arms and legs and enhanced her shapely figure.

She was a year younger than Benny. Her name was Olive, and she was John Swim's daughter — Benny's first cousin.

Olive Swim was an early bloomer, and soon realized that boys and men found her attractive. From the age of twelve she had a reputation as a flirt. She became the object of many a quarrel between jealous rivals. By the time Olive was seventeen, she was the object of Benny's affections. They had been living together, possibly sleeping together, in her father's cabin, and Benny considered Olive to be *his* girl.

William Guy Carr, a British-born writer who served for several years as a police officer in rural New Brunswick, wrote in his memoirs about the first time he encountered the Swim family. He and two companions were out deer hunting early one autumn morning, and stopped at John Swim's cabin. John and Olive were there, but not Benny. However, Benny was apparently lurking in the vicinity.

Olive made pancakes for the men for breakfast, and they contributed some ham and beans that they had in their car. One of the visitors, a man named Roy, thought that Olive was "making eyes" at him while they ate. After the meal, Carr and the other man headed into the woods, but Roy stayed behind. He said he would go into the forest at a different spot and drive deer toward them.

When Roy left the cabin a little later, Olive accompanied him, saying she'd like to get some partridges for supper. They got into the car and drove down an old wagon road. About a mile from the cabin, Roy stopped the car. They weren't there long when the crack of a rifle shattered the morning quiet.

Carr, who wasn't far away, heard the shot and hurried in

the direction of the sound, thinking one of his companions had bagged a deer. Instead, he found Roy's car, an ashen-faced Roy, and Olive. The two had been sitting in the car when a rifle bullet shattered the windshield and passed between them. Roy ducked under the dashboard for cover, but Olive jumped out and cried, "Benny! Benny! Don't shoot again!"

Fortunately, no one had been hurt. Olive had no doubt who had done the shooting. Although she was aware of Benny's possessiveness, she hadn't realized that jealousy could drive him to such fury.

Not long after that incident, John Swim moved to Benton to start a new farm. He left Olive and Benny living in his old cabin as "man and wife." Their relationship was stormy, and they lived a threadbare existence on Benny's meagre income. They moved in with Benny's parents in 1921. That was the year of a national census. To head off any suspicions he thought might arise concerning the family living arrangements, William Swim told the census taker that his niece was his daughter.

Life with Benny was suffocating for Olive, and she wanted out. In February of 1922, Benny asked Olive to marry him and presented her with a ring. To Benny's shock, she turned him down. She told him she was in love with another man.

It isn't known how Olive met Harvey Dixon Trenholm. He worked for a farmer named Sharp not far from her father's home near Benton. At age thirty-seven, Trenholm was much older than Olive, but he was tall and handsome, and had a sense of responsibility and a desire to get ahead that Benny lacked. Originally from Bayfield, Trenholm had been married previously. His wife died from illness, leaving him with a little daughter named Gladys.

In 1916, Trenholm enlisted with the Canadian Expeditionary Force. He left Gladys with his in-laws and went to fight on the Western Front. He survived the horrors of the trenches and returned home a decorated war hero. In Olive's eyes, Harvey Trenholm was everything Benny Swim wasn't. Moreover, he was her means of escape from the endless cycle of poverty in the Badlands.

After refusing Benny's proposal, Olive moved back in with her father. Benny went to Benton to try to see her, but this time Uncle John turned him away at the door. Benny returned home, sullen and angry. He felt betrayed by everyone he had trusted.

Meanwhile, Olive and Harvey's relationship was a whirlwind affair. On March 15, 1922, less than two months after they'd met, they were married in the Baptist church in Meductic. They had no honeymoon, but moved into a house on Sharp's farm. Trenholm had arranged to buy the property. Aside from his stint in the army, he had always been a farmer, and he expected to run a successful operation. Once he and his new wife were settled, he intended to bring Gladys home.

Olive's rejection devastated Benny. He told himself that Harvey Trenholm, an interfering outsider, had stolen his wife. In Benny's mind, that wasn't the sort of thing that any real man could turn his back on. He decided there would have to be a reckoning.

Benny sold some of his clothing to get money for train

fare. Then he traded his hunting rifle for a revolver. It was an old gun with a broken spring, but it would be easier to conceal under his coat than the rifle.

On March 27, 1922, Benny boarded a train for Woodstock. When he got off, he set out on foot for Benton, twelve miles away. A farmer named Alfred Ball picked him up in his wagon and gave him a ride part of the way. Benny told Ball that a man had taken his wife and he was looking into the matter.

After Ball dropped him off, Benny stopped at the home of Mrs. Jessie Kirk to ask for directions to the Sharp farm. When Mrs. Kirk asked why he was going there, Benny said that Olive and Trenholm had wronged him and he wanted to make things right. Mrs. Kirk advised her visitor to leave Olive and Harvey alone. As he left her house, she asked his name. He replied, "Benny Swim."

It was late afternoon with dusk setting in when Benny trudged through the snow up to the Sharp farm. He found a place to hide behind the barn from which he could watch the house. He might have been aware that Mr. Sharp had gone to town and only Olive and Harvey were home. Once or twice, he saw Olive pass by a window, wearing a familiar gingham dress. Standing in the chilly air, Benny began to shiver. The fingers clutching the gun were getting numb. Benny hoped that the faulty old weapon would work.

Then the door opened and Trenholm stepped outside with an axe in his hand. He went to the woodpile and began splitting logs. Benny waited until Trenholm had finished chopping and had gathered up an armload of firewood before he made his move.

Trenholm had almost reached the doorstep when Benny suddenly confronted him, gun in hand. Whatever words were exchanged between them would never be known. Benny shot Trenholm in the face from point-blank range. The soldier hero who had survived the hell of the Great War fell dead.

The sound of the gunshot brought Olive to the door. She flung it open, and there was Benny Swim pointing a gun at her. Benny begged Olive to come back to him. She said no, and Benny shot her in the breast.

The impact knocked Olive backwards into the kitchen. She turned and staggered across the room, trying to get away from Benny. He entered the house and shot her again. The bullet struck Olive in the back and pierced her heart, killing her on the spot.

Trying not to look at the body on the floor, Benny rummaged through the kitchen and found a notepad and pencil. He scribbled, "Goodbye Olive Swim. And sleep."

Having "made things right" with Olive and Trenholm, Benny left the house. He stumbled through the snow to the woods near a sheep pen behind the barn. There, he turned the gun on himself. He put the muzzle to his head and fired.

Hard-luck Benny couldn't even get suicide right. Perhaps his hand was shaking, or maybe it was because of the gun's broken spring, but the bullet didn't kill him. It struck his skull without penetrating the bone, furrowed under his skin, and stopped above his right eye.

Numb and bleeding, Benny made his way seven miles

through woods and snowy fields to the home of a farmer named J. Doherty. Sheriff Albion Foster found him there the next morning after following his blood-spattered trail. When Foster placed him under arrest, Benny said, "Sheriff, this is awful. I suppose I will hang for it."

Benny was taken to the Woodstock County jail. He said to the waiting reporters, "It's awful what a woman can bring a man to do." A doctor removed the bullet from his forehead.

Benny stood trial in Woodstock on April 27, 1922 before Chief Justice H.A. McKeown, the former counsellor who had defended Thomas Collins. Benny didn't deny shooting Olive and Harvey, but he did claim that Harvey had attacked him with the axe. Evidence documented at the crime scene disproved that. Benny was found guilty on two charges of first degree murder and was sentenced to hang on July 25, 1922.

Benny showed no emotion when Chief Justice McKeown condemned him to death, but when he was back in his cell, he suddenly began raving and had to be sedated. His defence counsel appealed on the grounds of insanity. He produced evidence that Benny's grandfather and mother were both mentally unbalanced. The execution was postponed so that Benny could undergo a psychiatric examination.

But the doctors concluded that Benny was not insane. They said the "fit" he'd displayed in his cell was an act. Benny's date with the hangman was rescheduled for September 15, 1922.

Benny seemed resigned to his fate. He gave the jail

guards no trouble. Then, on July 24, two fellow inmates, young men serving short sentences for petty crimes, told Sheriff Foster that Benny was planning to escape that very night. They said Benny told them he had managed to remove an iron plate from part of his cell. He was going to use it to knock out the lone night guard, take his keys, and break out. He had an escape route through the woods mapped out in his head and knew of a secluded cabin where he could hide until he could make a run for the Maine border.

Foster thought the story sounded incredible, but decided he'd better investigate. It was night, and Benny should have been asleep on his cot wearing only his underwear. Instead, Foster found him fully dressed. His pockets were stuffed with food he'd been hoarding from his meals. A search of his cell turned up the iron plate. Foster rewarded the informants by recommending that their sentences be reduced. This time, Benny owed his hard luck to his inability to keep his mouth shut.

Benny became morose after the failure of his escape attempt. He spoke to nobody except Reverend H.V. Bragdon, a spiritual advisor who visited him regularly. Benny revealed to the minister that his parents hadn't had him christened. So, on September 12, 1922, three days before he was to die, Benny was baptized in the corridor outside his cell.

What followed was a series of mishaps that could have been the inspiration for dark comedy, were it not such a cruel conclusion to the story of hard-luck Benny. When Benny was condemned to hang on July 25, 1922, Sheriff

Foster arranged for the official executioner, Arthur Ellis, to do the job. When the date was moved to September 15, Ellis informed Foster that he couldn't be in Woodstock that day due to another engagement. He advised Foster to contact J.D. Holmes, the man known in Canada as the Hangman's Assistant.

Holmes accepted the contract to execute Benny. On September 12, Foster received a telegram advising him that Holmes had broken his leg in an accident and couldn't make the trip to Woodstock.

Sheriff Foster was in a bind. In the absence of an executioner, it would be his duty to hang Benny, and he didn't want to do it. He had the execution postponed again, saying that he wasn't physically fit due to an automobile accident that had left him with a nervous condition.

The Department of Justice was obliged to advertise for a hangman. Applications came in from all over the country. Some included letters of reference as to the good character of the applicant. One young man even included a photograph of himself.

Sheriff Foster chose two Montreal men: M.A. Doyle and F.G. Gill. Both were recommended by the sheriff of Montreal as experienced, reliable men. Doyle was to be the executioner, and Gill would be on hand should he require assistance. October 6, 1922 was the date for the hanging. There would be no more postponements. Hard-luck Benny spent his last days suffering from tonsillitis.

At five o'clock in the morning on October 6, Doyle and Gill took Benny from his cell and handcuffed him. They walked him to the gallows accompanied by Deputy Sheriff

Hedley Mooers. Benny prayed the whole time.

Doyle positioned Benny on the trap door, put a black hood over his head, and placed the noose around his neck. Benny was in the middle of reciting the Lord's Prayer when Doyle sprang the trap. Benny plunged into the pit below.

After two or three minutes, Doyle, Gill, Mooers, and three doctors entered the area below the scaffold. Benny was hanging with his feet about a foot above the ground. One of the doctors began to check to be sure there was no sign of life, when Doyle suddenly ordered, "Cut him down. He's dead as a doornail."

Mooers supported Benny while Gill cut the rope. He was carried to a corridor and laid on a cot. The doctors listened to Benny's chest and felt his wrists and were startled to find that Benny was still alive. His neck hadn't been broken, and he hadn't been left hanging long enough to asphyxiate.

No one knew what to do. Minutes passed, and Benny began to wheeze. Someone said it was only a death rattle. But the doctors found Benny's pulse growing stronger and his breathing improving. It was just a matter of time before he regained consciousness.

Almost an hour passed before Doyle was told he would have to carry out the execution again. It was only then that Mooers and the others realized that Doyle was drunk. They turned the job over to Gill and warned him not to make a mess of it.

Gill and Mooers carried Benny back to the gallows. Gill put a noose around his neck and dropped him — this time his neck was broken. The body was left hanging for nineteen minutes before the doctors officially pronounced Benny dead.

News of the botched hanging sparked public outrage. An official commission was organized to look into the sorry affair and the manner in which capital punishment was administered in Canada. Benny Swim's ordeal on the gallows drew considerable public sympathy, something he'd had little of in life. The only man in Canada known to have been hanged twice, he was hard-luck Benny to the very end.

13

Ulysses Lauzon: Bad Day at the Races

Prince Edward Island society has had to deal with the sort of criminal activities that plague communities everywhere: burglaries, hold-ups, assaults, fraud. All of the wrongdoings that keep police departments busy. But the island is not usually associated with bank-robbing gangsters in the mould of America's John Dillinger, or Canada's own infamous bandit, Edwin Boyd. However, one day in 1945, Island police stood in a life-and-death confrontation with the most-wanted men in Canada. One was Ulysses Lauzon, a thug who considered himself a master criminal.

Uly Lauzon, of Windsor, Ontario, never wanted to be anything but a crook. He said so to a psychologist during one of his numerous incarcerations. He was proud of his criminal exploits and hated the idea of working for a living. He was determined to never be a "wage slave" like his law-abiding father.

Lauzon began his outlaw career early, stealing money

and anything else he wanted. He was fifteen when a judge declared him "incorrigible" and sent him to reform school for a year. But the tough discipline did nothing to change Lauzon's anti-social attitude. After his release, he resumed his thieving ways, adding auto theft to his criminal repertoire. He was caught again and sentenced to two years in the Ontario Reformatory in Guelph. Lauzon boasted that one day he'd make it to the federal penitentiary in Kingston. His dream soon came true.

Three months after entering "the joint" in Guelph, Lauzon escaped with three other inmates. They headed straight for Windsor. Police soon tracked them to a garage there and surrounded the building. The fugitives made a break for it, with Lauzon at the wheel of a stolen car. He caught officers by surprise by crashing the car through the garage doors, but smashed into a police vehicle. With six officers pointing guns at them, Lauzon and his friends surrendered.

For escaping custody, Lauzon was sentenced to two years in the Kingston pen, where he would also have to serve the remainder of his initial term. He was not yet twenty years old. Lauzon had no regrets. As far as he was concerned, prison was a crime school where he could learn from professionals.

Kingston Pen was Canada's Big House, where the most dangerous criminals were incarcerated. In prison hierarchy, the elite were the bandits who pulled daring armed robberies. Lauzon admired them and listened to their stories about big jobs and the easy life that stolen money could buy. Reforming never occurred to him.

Lauzon was released in December 1944. On February

23, 1945, he and three other hoodlums robbed a bank in Windsor at gunpoint. The swag was only eight hundred and thirty dollars, but Uly was thrilled. He had pulled off his first armed robbery.

But his excitement was short-lived. Five days later, Lauzon and accomplice Joe Poireau, nineteen years old, were arrested in Windsor. A judge released them on bail of ten thousand dollars each. Lauzon made good use of the time to sabotage the Crown's case against him.

The Crown's principal witness was twenty-year-old Eileen Cornell, and Lauzon set out to woo the impressionable young woman. He cut an exciting, dashing figure, and seduced her with promises of big money and the high life. Eileen fell for Uly like Bonnie fell for Clyde. On March 26, 1945, they were married. According to the law of the time, a wife couldn't be compelled to testify against her husband. Unable to put Eileen on the witness stand, the Crown had no case. Lauzon was acquitted. Poireau simply failed to appear in court.

On May 9, Lauzon graduated to the major leagues of armed robbery when he and Poireau hit the Canadian Bank of Commerce in the village of Ayr in Waterloo County. In a heist that would have impressed Dillinger or Boyd, Poireau stood guard with a gun while Lauzon ordered staff and customers to crawl under counters. The robbers escaped with almost twenty thousand dollars in cash and more than fifty-three thousand in negotiable bonds. It was the first major crime pulled off by the bandits dubbed the Detroit River Gang by the press.

The outlaws didn't get much chance to enjoy the loot.

Within a week, the Ontario Provincial Police arrested Lauzon and locked him in Kitchener's Waterloo County Jail. Police took Poireau by surprise in a Winnipeg hotel room. He soon joined Lauzon in Kitchener.

The big-time robbery gave Lauzon the kind of notoriety he craved. The guards decided that he and Poireau could best be watched if they were kept together. They were lodged in cells in the same corridor and permitted to take their daily visit to the exercise yard together. That was a mistake because it allowed them to plot an escape.

Somehow, Lauzon and Poireau obtained hacksaw blades. Early in the morning of July 18, 1945, they cut their way out of their cells, got past a supposedly "escape-proof" steel door, squeezed through a tiny second-floor window, crept along the top of the jail yard wall, and slid down a streetlight pole to freedom. By the time a guard found their cells empty, they were long gone.

Lauzon and Poireau stayed a jump ahead of the police by stealing cars, frequently abandoning one that got too "hot" and replacing it with another. They kept to backroads as they criss-crossed southwestern Ontario, pulling petty robberies for money to live on. They connected with a thirty-year-old Windsor hoodlum named Walter Koresky. He provided the guns they needed to get back into business.

With Koresky as a new member, the Detroit River Gang struck the Canadian Bank of Commerce in Port Perry, Ontario, on August 6, 1945. Koresky sat at the wheel of the stolen getaway car while Lauzon and Poireau, masked and brandishing revolvers, burst in and ordered everyone to drop to the floor. The bandits roared away with more than twenty-eight hundred dollars.

The haul wasn't big, but it was enough for the gang to set themselves up in a cabin in the woods north of Chicoutimi, Quebec. Lauzon intended to use this isolated hideout as a base from which his gang could rob banks in Ontario and Quebec. He was so certain the police would never find it that he had his pregnant wife Eileen join him there.

The gang's next target was the Royal Bank of Canada in the little community of Bath, near Kingston. They hit it on August 20. Once again, Koresky drove the getaway car. When Lauzon and Poireau went in with guns in hand, they didn't even bother to wear masks. They emerged with ten thousand dollars in cash and over three hundred and fifty thousand in negotiable bonds. Lauzon must have been ecstatic when the newspapers said it was the biggest haul ever taken in a bank robbery in Canada.

With ten thousand dollars of ready money in hand, the gang could have lain low and fenced the bonds on the black market. But Lauzon wasn't the professional he thought he was. He and Poireau made several trips to Montreal banks to cash in the bonds themselves.

On August 31, 1945, Poireau went into a Royal Bank branch in downtown Montreal with six thousand dollars in Victory Bonds. Bank employee Hatton Longshaw recognized the serial numbers from a list of stolen bonds that had been issued by police. Poireau sensed Longshaw's suspicion and pulled a gun. He ordered Longshaw to get on the floor. Instead, Longshaw grabbed a revolver from a drawer. Fortunately for him, Poireau didn't shoot. Instead, he ran for the door. Just as he reached it, Longshaw shot him. The bullet severed Poireau's spine, crippling him for life.

Lauzon, who had been waiting outside in a stolen car, fled. He managed to slip past a police dragnet that sealed off the Island of Montreal. Lauzon was certain that if Poireau wasn't dead, he would talk, so he sped to the cabin to get Koresky and Eileen before police arrived.

The gang headed east. Travelling backroads in a series of stolen cars, they crossed Quebec, New Brunswick, and Nova Scotia. Meanwhile, police departments across Canada and in American border cities were put on alert to be on the lookout for the Detroit River Gang, who were armed and dangerous. The police communications didn't include photographs of the suspects.

Sometime in the first week of September, the fugitives took the ferry from Cape Tormentine, New Brunswick, to Borden, Prince Edward Island. Their car, stolen in Quebec City, had New Brunswick licence plates, which were soon replaced with Quebec plates. In the trunk was an assortment of stolen Canadian and American plates.

On September 7, 1945, three strangers drove into Cavendish and stopped at a tourist home owned by Mrs. A (who did not want her name to appear in newspapers). They wanted to rent a cabin, and smilingly told her, "We're going to be your star boarders."

Mrs. A said she rented rooms only, but there were cabins nearby on property owned by Reverend C (who also preferred not to be identified in the press). He was in

Charlottetown at the moment but was due back anytime. She told the visitors they were welcome to wait for him on the lawn.

When Reverend C arrived, he cheerfully rented the visitors a double cabin, pleased to have guests in the off-season. He arranged for them to have their meals in Mrs. A's dining room. The visitors registered as Mr. and Mrs. Joseph Jensen of Halifax, and John Charles Kerr from Hamilton, Ontario.

The three guests were pleasant enough and charmed everyone they met. But Mrs. A soon sensed something suspicious about them. For one thing, why were people who said they were from Nova Scotia and Ontario touring in a car with Quebec plates? And why did they always park their car behind a screen of trees out of sight of the road? It seemed odd that, although Kerr was the older of the two men, he took instructions from the boyish-looking Jensen. Kerr's behaviour actually struck Mrs. A as juvenile.

It was evident to Mrs. A that Eileen Jensen was pregnant, though the young woman did not yet show much of a bump. Eileen always wore dark glasses and seemed to be moody and nervous. One evening she excused herself from the supper table four times without explanation. Several times, Mrs. A heard Eileen crying in the cabin.

Reverend C enjoyed the company of his guests and played golf with the men. They gave him an expensive cigarette lighter as a gift. A young woman named Jennie who worked for Mrs. A as a waitress and maid was also much taken with the visitors, especially after Jensen and Kerr drove her to Charlottetown where they bought her a new dress and coat and treated her to a fun evening at a dance hall.

Mrs. A kept her suspicions to herself in case they turned out to be groundless. But she was concerned that the strangers might be trying to convince Jennie to go with them when they finally left. She forbade Jennie to accompany them to Charlottetown again.

After a couple of days, the visitors must have realized that Mrs. A was uneasy because Koresky became her shadow. Wherever she went, he found an excuse to go along, whether it was to Rustico where she bought groceries or to her brother's nearby farm where she milked the cows twice a day. Koresky spent a lot of time in Mrs. A's house. He seemed lonely and restless and talked a lot. In one unguarded moment, he let slip that his name was Walter.

Lauzon appeared to be genuinely enjoying himself, spending hours talking to residents of Cavendish and taking trips to Charlottetown where he spent money freely. But Koresky was bored. He asked Mrs. A, "What's to do around here?"

She told him about the harness races upcoming at the Covehead track. She knew something about the horses and offered tips on good bets. Lauzon liked the idea of a day at the races, and asked Mrs. A to go with them. She declined the invitation. Then she found a diplomatic reason to say no when Lauzon asked if they could borrow her radio and take it to their cabin. That turned out to be a lucky break for the law.

On the visitors' fourth day in Cavendish, Jennie turned the radio on while she and Mrs. A did housework. They heard a news bulletin that struck Mrs. A with a chill. It told of two armed and dangerous criminals accompanied by a woman who had last been seen in Quebec and were thought to be heading east. The descriptions fit the Jensens and Kerr.

It didn't seem to dawn on Jennie that her new friends could be the fugitives. Mrs. A said nothing to her, in case she might inadvertently warn them. But she felt she had to tell somebody. The following day, September 12, 1945, she confided in Arthur Brown, an officer from the Royal Canadian Air Force base in Summerside who was one of her guests.

After listening to Mrs. A's story, Brown said they should inform Reverend C immediately. The reverend was about to deliver a radio to the cabin when they intercepted him. He was shocked at the idea that such nice young people could be criminals. He was afraid of what the consequences might be if he and Mrs. A accused innocent people. He was also concerned for their reputations in the tourist business.

Mrs. A convinced Reverend C to drive Brown to the Royal Canadian Mounted Police headquarters in Charlottetown. The police would know what to do. When Brown reported to the police that afternoon, he told them the Jensens and Kerr were at the Covehead races.

The two constables dispatched to Covehead were veterans of the force, but had not been in Prince Edward Island long. Constable T.C. Keefe, thirty years old and a native of Edmonton, Alberta, had been a Mountie for seven years. He had been posted to Charlottetown just three weeks earlier, following duty in the Arctic.

Constable W.H. Warren, thirty-five years old, was from St. John, New Brunswick. He had joined the Royal Canadian Mounted Police ten years earlier, but had spent five years overseas with the Canadian Army. He had been in Prince Edward Island for only two months. Warren was a physically powerful man who came from a family of boxers. His grandfather had fought world heavyweight champion John L. Sullivan.

Warren and Keefe arrived at the track just before the last race and spotted the suspects coming from the exit. They stopped them and asked to see their driver's registrations. The documents the men presented identified them as Joseph Jensen and John Charles Kerr, but the constables weren't satisfied with the answers they gave to a few questions. They told the three they'd have to accompany them to Charlottetown. Since the suspects were not under arrest, the constables didn't search them for weapons or handcuff them.

Lauzon knew that the Mounties would soon learn who he was. He had no intention of going back to prison. When they left the racetrack, he was at the wheel of his car with Eileen sitting beside him. Warren was in the back seat. Keefe followed in the police car with Koresky in the back.

About four miles down the dirt road, Lauzon suddenly floored the accelerator. The car shot forward and hit ninety miles per hour. Lauzon lost control on a sharp curve, and the car came to a jolting stop in a ditch. Eileen's head struck the windshield. She stumbled out and fell to the ground as though she fainted. Warren immediately jumped out and knelt beside her to give first aid. As she came to, the constable looked up and saw Lauzon standing over him with a revolver pointed at his head.

Meanwhile, the police car stopped, and Keefe rushed up to the ditched car. Behind him, Koresky got out. He had a gun in his hand.

The Mounties seemed to be at the outlaws' mercy. Lauzon ordered them to lie face down on the ground. Instead, Warren stood up and told Lauzon not to do anything foolish.

Suddenly Warren lunged, catching Lauzon by surprise. Lauzon pulled the trigger four times, but the hammer snapped uselessly. Warren smashed him in the head with a left hook and a right cross that knocked him sprawling and sent the gun flying from his hand.

Koresky was still armed, but the hand holding the gun trembled. Keefe carefully edged his way toward him. Eileen, fully recovered from her "faint," looked on fearfully.

Lauzon scrambled across the ground after his gun, but Warren pounced on him. As they struggled, Lauzon repeatedly cried to Koresky, "Shoot the bastard! Shoot him in the head!"

Keefe warned Koresky not to shoot or he'd hang for murder. Warren shouted to Keefe to grab Koresky; his gun wasn't loaded. Koresky snarled, "Isn't it?" and fired a shot that missed Warren.

Before Koresky could shoot again, Warren seized Lauzon in his arms and lifted him off the ground, using him as a shield. A second later, Koresky fired, the bullet whistling past Warren's head. Keefe was now close enough to tackle

Koresky. As he did, Warren threw Lauzon to the ground and grabbed his gun.

Still clutching his pistol, Koresky struggled. Lauzon again urged him to shoot. Warren told Lauzon to shut up, or he'd beat him to death. Koresky realized the game was up and dropped his gun. Police later found that Lauzon's gun had failed to discharge because the "professional" criminal had loaded it with the wrong ammunition.

Lauzon, Koresky, and Eileen were locked up in the Charlottetown jail. They had thousands of dollars in cash. The capture of the Detroit River Gang in Prince Edward Island made headlines across Canada. With his usual bravado, Lauzon told reporters that the Mounties who'd captured him "sure had guts." He said that if Koresky hadn't gotten "cold feet," they could have killed both constables and dumped their bodies overboard on their way back to the mainland. When a reporter asked Lauzon if he'd planned on robbing a bank in Charlottetown, he sneered, "You have no bank worth robbing." He boasted that he'd escape again and had money stashed where no one would ever find it.

Warren and Keefe were awarded the King's Police and Fire Services Medal for bravery in the line of duty. Eileen was soon released from custody. Her child died within a few days of birth. Lauzon and Koresky were sent to the Kingston Penitentiary: Koresky for fifteen years and Lauzon for thirty-five. An editorial in Summerside's *Journal Pioneer* quipped, "That should serve them a lesson to keep away from the races."

Less than two years later, Lauzon escaped from Kingston

Pen along with Ottawa hoodlum Nick Minnelli and no-torious Toronto criminal Mickey McDonald. Using a plan believed to have been conceived by Lauzon, the three went over the prison wall on the night of August 16, 1947. Minnelli was recaptured eight months later. He was the lucky one.

McDonald was never heard from again and was believed to have been murdered in the United States. There were no doubts about Lauzon's fate. His bullet-riddled corpse was found in a Mississippi swamp on July 19, 1948. Police believed Lauzon had run afoul of local gangsters.

Lauzon's gruesome end proved that he was not the archcriminal of his own imagination, but a two-bit punk who got in way over his head. An editor of *The Guardian* in Charlottetown wrote of Lauzon's demise, "The master strategist created a Frankenstein which liquidated him."

Bibliography

Books and Essays

Anderson, Frank W. *A Dance with Death: Canadian Women on the Gallows 1754–1954.* Saskatoon & Calgary: Fifth House, 1996.

Cook, Matthew. "Murder or Suicide? The Mysterious Death of Edie Brailsford, Dominion, 1923." Lecture, Cape Breton Centre for Heritage and Science, Sydney, NS, February 25, 2010.

De Villiers, Marq and Sheila Hirtle. *A Dune Adrift: The Strange Origins and Curious History of Sable Island.* Toronto: McClelland & Stewart, 2004.

Dictionary of Canadian Biography. Toronto: University of Toronto and Université Laval.

Fingard, Judith. *The Dark Side of Life in Victorian Halifax.* Porters Lake, NS: Pottersfield Press, 1989.

Fryer, Mary Beacock. *More Battlefields of Canada.* Toronto: Dundurn, 1993.

Graham, Monica. *The Great Maritime Detective: The Exploits and Adventures of the Notorious Peachie Carroll.* Halifax: Nimbus Publishing, 2009.

Grant, B.J. *Six for the Hangman.* Fredericton: Goose Lane Editions, 1983.

Hennigar, Ted R. *The Rum Running Years.* Hantsport, NS: Lancelot Press, 1984.

Keefe, Rose. *The Man Who Got Away: The Bugs Moran Story: A Biography.* Nashville, TN: Cumberland House, 2005.

MacDonald, M.A. *Fortune & La Tour: The Civil War in Acadia.* Toronto: Methuen, 1983.

MacIntyre, N. Carroll. *The Life and Adventures of Detective Peter Owen Carroll.* Antigonish, NS: Sundown Publications, 1985.

McSherry, Peter. *What Happened to Mickey? The Life and Death of Donald "Mickey" McDonald, Public Enemy No. 1.* Toronto: Dundurn, 2013.

Paterson, T.W. *Canadian Battles & Massacres: 300 Years of Warfare and Atrocities on Canadian Soil.* Langley, BC: Stagecoach Publications, 1977.

Pfeifer, Jeffrey and Ken Leyton-Brown. *Death by Rope: An Anthology of Canadian Executions,* Regina: Vanity Press, 2007.

Randell, Captain Jack & Meigs O. Frost. *I'm Alone.* Indianapolis IN: Bobbs-Merrill Company, 1930.

Rannie, William F. *Saint Pierre and Miquelon.* Lincoln, ON: Rannie Publications Limited, 1963.

Saunders, Kenneth. *The Rectory Murder: The Mysterious Crime that Shocked Turn-of-the-Century New Brunswick.* Toronto: James Lorimer & Co., 1989.

Willoughby, Malcolm F. *Rum War at Sea.* Washington, D.C.: Treasury Dept., US Coast Guard, 1964.

Newspapers
Charlottetown *Guardian*
Halifax *Morning Chronicle*
North Sydney *Herald*
Sydney *Post*
Toronto *Globe*

Acknowledgements

The author would like to thank the following for their kind and invaluable assistance: the provincial archives of New Brunswick, Nova Scotia and Prince Edward Island; the Beaton Institute, Cape Breton University; the Cape Breton Centre for Heritage and Science, Sydney, NS; the Vaughan, Ontario Public Library; Penumbra Press, Newcastle, Ontario; James Lorimer and the people at Formac Publishing; Matthew Cook, and as always, the staff at the Guelph, Ontario, Public Library. A Special note of thanks to fellow historian Rose Keefe.

Index